Back on Track

Back on Track

SOUND TRANSIT'S FIGHT TO SAVE LIGHT RAIL

Bob Wodnik

WSU
PRESS

Washington State University Press
Pullman, Washington

WSU PRESS
WASHINGTON STATE UNIVERSITY

Washington State University Press
PO Box 645910
Pullman, Washington 99164-5910
Phone: 800-354-7360
Email: wsupress@wsu.edu
Website: wsupress.wsu.edu

Library of Congress Cataloging-in-Publication Data

Names: Wodnik, Bob, 1954- author.
Title: Back on track : Sound Transit's fight to save light rail / Bob Wodnik.
Description: Pullman, Washington : Washington State University Press, 2019. |
    Includes bibliographical references and index.
Identifiers: LCCN 2019015008 | ISBN 9780874223699 (acid-free paper)
Subjects: LCSH: Central Puget Sound Regional Transit Authority (Wash.) |
    Street-railroads--Washington (State)--Seattle.
Classification: LCC HE4491.S433 C46 2019 | DDC 388.4/6097977--dc23
        LC record available at https://lccn.loc.gov/2019015008

Cover photo courtesy of Sound Transit.

Contents

Maps and Illustrations

Preface

Although its formal existence only dates back to 1996, a mere child as established transit agencies go, Sound Transit's early life is remembered as much for its conflicts as its achievements.

Since the late 1960s, the Seattle region has fought over light rail transit, its enormous cost, and undetermined benefits. Many believed then and remain convinced to this day that expanded busways, freeways, carpools, and bike lanes are a better solution to urban congestion. Even now with 22 miles up and running between the University of Washington and Sea-Tac Airport and a voter-approved $54 billion expansion of the light rail system underway, the battle lines remain tightly drawn. Eventually, Central Puget Sound will have a 116-mile-long light rail system that connects the region's major cities. But conflict, cost increases, and delays mean the time it takes to build out the light rail line, already decades into the future, could stretch out even further, creating more unrest in the increasingly traffic-clogged Seattle region.

But this book is not about current controversies. Those stories await the eyes of future historians.

Instead, *Back on Track: Sound Transit's Fight to Save Light Rail* explores the early battles over bringing light rail to the Seattle area, its near demise in the pivotal year of 2001, and the subsequent fight, led by CEO Joni Earl, to keep it on track. Back then there was legitimate concern that the fledgling agency would simply disappear and along with it the plan to build the region's multi-billion dollar light rail system.

Sound Transit was born of controversy—so what? Why tell that story? I was encouraged and then convinced of its worth by longtime friends and Sound Transit colleagues, Tom Suarez, Rebecca Roush, and Gloria Hatch, who said the story ought to be told not just for now but for the future, for all those transit riders who would otherwise have no idea how close Sound Transit came to the brink. At the very least, they pointed out, it would make an interesting read for the scores of new Sound Transit employees who might otherwise have scant knowledge of their agency's origin.

As a former writer for Sound Transit and its then CEO Joni Earl, I was in a perfect position to tell Sound Transit's early history. I had access to the inner workings of the agency, its meetings, emails, documents, and thoughts of its leaders.

To stitch together the story I interviewed dozens of current and former Sound Transit employees, board members, community leaders, and critics. I spent hours interviewing Joni Earl, starting with her principles of leadership and ideas for managing in crisis before branching out to explore the influences in her life and her childhood in Bremerton, Washington, an hour's ferry ride across Puget Sound from downtown Seattle. Hers is a unique story of an amazingly successful woman who won big in the male-dominated transit industry.

Invaluable aid in my research came from the public affairs consulting firm Cocker Fennessy, which provided hundreds of documents and records from their years working for Sound Transit. In addition, the region's many newspapers, at that time healthy and fully staffed, provided insight into the day-to-day thinking and events of the time. As a former reporter, I also found the newspaper record a sobering reminder of how much that industry has changed since 2000.

Together, those sources tell the important early episodes that shaped Sound Transit's growth from an agency of 23 employees to one pushing 1,000. Although the debate about light rail continues to this day, there is no longer serious talk about dissolving Sound Transit and moving on. Those days are now part of the colorful history of Sound Transit and its place in the transportation life of the Pacific Northwest.

—Bob Wodnik

———

Note about Citations
In the interest of readability, citations for interviews are provided on first appearance only. Subsequent quotes from the same sources are not cited. Documents not otherwise cited come from Sound Transit archives.

The Major Players

DAVID BEAL: Director of Planning and Development. Sound Transit employee, 1996–2015.

DESMOND BROWN: Sound Transit General Counsel, 1997–present.

SHEILA DEZARN: Government Relations Manager. Sound Transit employee, 1996–2007.

BOB DREWEL: Snohomish County Executive, 1992–2004; Puget Sound Regional Council Executive Director, 2004–2014; Sound Transit Board Chair, 1996–1998.

JONI EARL: Sound Transit CEO, 2001–2016.

DAVE EARLING: Edmonds Mayor 2011–present; Edmonds City Council 1992–2003; Sound Transit Board Chair, 2000–2002; Sound Transit Board Member 1996–2003; 2011–present.

AHMAD FAZEL: Executive Director Link light rail, 2002–2018.

ANNE FENNESSY: founding member of Cocker Fennessy, Sound Transit's public affairs consultant.

AGNES GOVERN: Executive Director ST Express regional bus service, 1997–2009.

TIM HEALY: Director of Marketing. Sound Transit employee, 1996–present.

RIC ILGENFRITZ: Communications Director and Planning Director. Sound Transit employee, 2001–2017.

RON LEWIS: Executive Director Link light rail. Sound Transit consultant, 1998–2002. Sound Transit employee, 2002–present.

PAUL MATSUOKA: Deputy Executive Director. Sound Transit employee, 1996–2007.

BRIAN MCCARTAN: Finance Director. Sound Transit employee, 1997–2018.

ROB MCKENNA: Washington State Attorney General, 2004–2012; King County Council Member, 1996–2004; Sound Transit Board Member, 1996–2001.

GREG NICKELS: Mayor of Seattle, 2002–2010; Sound Transit Board Chair, 2008–2010.

RON SIMS: King County Executive, 1997–2009; Sound Transit Board Member, 1997–2009; Sound Transit Board Chair 2002–2004.

MIKE VASKA: Seattle attorney and Seattle Chamber of Commerce leader.

BOB WHITE: Executive Director. Sound Transit employee, 1996–2001.

Introduction

It really was a 14-mile-long community party.
—Rebecca Roush, Sound Transit employee
at the Link light rail launch

Saturday, July 18, 2009—Crowds began forming long before the first trains arrived. Parents waited patiently as their wide-eyed children watched the colorful jugglers, musicians, clowns, and magicians work their magic. Near the International District Station in Seattle's Chinatown, lion dancers snaked alongside the customers waiting in line. At the underground Westlake Station, a musician strummed a guitar while singing "My Darling Clementine." Not far away, a clown in a pink polka-dot dress directed three women toward the station's crowded platform: "Ladies, there's a train with your name on it."

But on this sunny Saturday morning the clowns and jugglers were strictly sideshow: the main event was the sparkling new blue and white light rail trains. Those first Link passengers, some wearing shorts and sunglasses, others in hijabs and dashikis, years later would tell their friends they'd been there when light rail finally arrived. Before the weekend was over nearly 100,000 people visited the 12 stations and rode Link trains 14 miles between downtown and the last station stop in the City of Tukwila.

"Just like a real city," one rider marveled.

Just 10 years earlier, in the late 1990s, who would have thought this day would ever arrive?

Little did those waiting that July day seem to care that only eight years earlier the light rail project had nearly collapsed without one foot of track being laid. Then opponents had doubled down their efforts to kill the project and every day, it seemed, a headline in local papers mocked the "hapless," the "beleaguered," the "out of control" Sound Transit.

The small transit agency headquartered in Seattle had survived in those early years on a steady diet of controversy, perhaps not surprising given the size and enormous cost of its light rail program.

Providing ammunition to its many critics, the agency's early stumbles made it appear as if it couldn't get out of its own way.

The Sound Transit staffers who organized the opening weekend of entertainment and free train rides were amazed at the joyous spirit that swept through the crowds. At times spontaneous shouts erupted as trains burst through the Beacon Hill Tunnel and into the brilliant summer sunshine. One rider, originally from New York, joked to a Sound Transit volunteer that "I'll know Seattle is a big city for real when I see a rat in that tunnel."

• • •

Those who had played major roles in the long-running drama to bring light rail to Central Puget Sound had their own thoughts on opening day.

As packed trains flew by the Columbia City Station, Ahmad Fazel, the Link executive director whose indefatigable presence guided the light rail department back from the brink, sat alone under the shade of a tree as if collecting his thoughts. Few were more invested in the success of this weekend than Fazel, who during the bleakest days had staked his reputation that trains would be running in 2009.

Greg Nickels, the mayor of Seattle who took punches for light rail as long as anyone could remember, felt cathartic as he traveled from station to station greeting passengers. "All the pain and agony, the sleepless nights, it felt like ok, it was worth it," he would later say.[1]

Mike Vaska, the Seattle attorney and Chamber of Commerce leader who was a stalwart for light rail in business and political circles before there even was a Sound Transit, was philosophical. "It's just one of these life lessons. If you really think something is important you keep working at it. So many points along the way this thing could have failed, I could have looked back and said we did all that work and I learned stuff but nothing came of it. But here's an investment that will serve this community for generations."[2]

Finally, there was Joni Earl, who perhaps more than anyone was responsible for turning the agency around and finally bringing trains to transit-starved Puget Sound. Wearing a lime green pullover shirt like all Sound Transit employees wore that first day, she could have been anyone from Sound Transit working the crowd and answering questions. As she rode from station to station she wore a smile so genuine and spontaneous it seemed to burst forth from a wellspring deep inside her.

For Earl, it was a moment of personal and professional triumph. Nine years earlier she'd accepted a high-level job at Sound Transit just as the light rail program was teetering on collapse and in those crisis-filled first years many wondered if the fledgling agency would survive.

Looking back, Earl shuddered at the crazy uncertainty that tested her like nothing else. There were times when she brought several days' worth of clothes to work because she was literally living in Sound Transit's Seattle headquarters. There were countless trips to Washington, D.C., to soothe anxious Congressional leaders whose reputations rode on the success of Sound Transit. There were unrelenting attacks from all corners: legal, political, personal. The city's largest newspaper, the *Seattle Times*, printed a headline urging the region to "Face Reality, Pull Plug on Light Rail."[3] Thirty miles north of Seattle, the *Everett Herald* wondered: "Sound Transit—On the Midnight Train to Nowhere?"[4]

There was rancor at public meetings as angry taxpayers lined up for their turn to eviscerate the agency's leaders. Democrat Booth Gardner, a former two-term governor, wanted to kill light rail and said so to anyone who would listen. Dino Rossi, a prominent Republican state senator and later two-time candidate for governor, introduced a bill in the legislature asking voters to dissolve Sound Transit. A Seattle City Council member put forth a city resolution, laced with anti-Sound Transit barbs, that would have scrapped light rail. Lawsuit after lawsuit sought to drive the final nail into Sound Transit. And so it went in the early days as months stretched to years.

In some ways, Earl's life was pointing to this moment in July 2009. Her long career in public management helped her recognize and develop the skills necessary to lead through crisis. And there was never more crisis than when she started at Sound Transit and discovered the desperate need for someone to pull it through.

During those days, sometimes existing only on strength of will, Joni Earl and her team at Sound Transit came to define the future of transportation in Central Puget Sound.

1

The Holy Grail of Transit

Rail was always the holy grail of transit.
—Tim Healy, Sound Transit marketing director

The quest for rail transit in Seattle began more than a century ago.

Seattle is a slender hourglass of a city, bounded on the west by the Puget Sound shoreline and on the east by 22-mile-long Lake Washington. But for all its scenic wonders, urban lakes, forested parks, valleys, steep hills, and unspoiled beaches with their bald eagles and barking sea lions, Seattle cannot hide its ugly transportation history.

The fledgling city was first built on rail, dating back to 1889 when electric streetcars began running. Seattle's population was about 43,000 and in those days its streets were often a monsoon mess, making steel tracks a smart upgrade to the city's core. Thirty years later, the City of Seattle took ownership of the streetcar system and by 1936 operated 410 streetcars on 26 electric routes, as well as three cable car lines totaling 231 miles of track. The city also ran 60 gasoline-powered buses on 18 routes.[1]

Those streetcars, however, couldn't survive the automobile evolution. A hint of Seattle's all-bus, all-car future came in 1932 when the state refused to include streetcar tracks when it built the Aurora Bridge connecting the Queen Anne and Fremont neighborhoods. A further blow came in 1940 when the federal government loaned the city $10 million to be used, in part, to pay for a new bus system. Ready or not, rubber wheels were in and steel-wheeled streetcars out.

From the April morning in 1941 when Seattle's last streetcar rolled into the Freemont car barn until Link light rail began running that sunny July day 68 years later, a generation of Puget Sounders grew up and retired without ever stepping onto a transit train.

Over the decades various attempts were made to move the city and surrounding region back on track, but once the streetcar tracks were torn up and paved over for cars and buses, the return to rail was like pushing a locomotive uphill. The era of lost elections and shelved transit train studies had begun.

Rail was first officially snubbed in February 1968 when King County voters approved parts of a "Forward Thrust" tax measure to pay for a diverse assortment of improvements. Those improvements included parks, sewers, housing, roads, and the giant concrete mushroom called the Kingdome, where for years the Seattle Mariners and Seattle Seahawks would toil far from the bright lights of glory. In 1968, when a round-trip flight to Alaska was $48 and a West Seattle view home was available for $20,000, the yearly tax increase to pay for the Forward Thrust investments in sewers and parks ended up costing the average homeowner about $6.47.

But the Forward Thrust bond proposal that would have brought modern rapid transit trains and buses to Seattle received 51 percent of the votes on that 1968 ballot, a long reach from the 60 percent needed to pass. Even back then the battle lines over light rail were clearly drawn.

Jim Ellis, the ubiquitous Seattle community leader and architect behind Forward Thrust, blamed "rifle shooting by opponents," for transit's defeat.[2] He was referencing "Citizens for Sensible Transit" led by Vic Gould, a Seattle real estate broker. In what would become the opposition's mantra for the next 50 years, Gould said rail transit was an open-ended money grab for a system that would not reduce automobile traffic more than 3 percent.[3]

For transit supporters, it was back to the drawing board. Two years later, in 1970, rail transit again appeared before voters. But in those two years, Seattle had changed. Just eight years removed from the 1962 World's Fair, the city's unabashedly optimistic coming-out party, the region was suffering through a hard Boeing bust.

Boeing, Seattle's giant aerospace company, first sprang up on the banks of the Duwamish River in 1916 and fifty years later was the engine that made the city soar. But following decades of prosperity and growth, Boeing suffered a major economic slump in the early 1970s and its workforce shrank from 83,700 in 1968 to 20,750 in 1971. As a consequence, Seattle's population of about 530,000 began shrinking. So many people pulled up roots it seemed as if household movers were the only companies doing well. The blows were felt in other, more extreme ways, including a dramatic increase in the suicide rate. To ward off jumpers, an anti-suicide net was eventually installed high up the city's iconic Space Needle.[4]

In this atmosphere of fear, voters were more worried about their jobs than increasing taxes to pay for mass transit. Who needed a train for a job that no longer existed?

This time, the Forward Thrust transit measure mustered only 46 percent yes votes and the $900 million in federal aid earmarked for Seattle instead went south to build Atlanta's MARTA rail system.

Jim Ellis, who again led the charge for mass transit, was bitterly disappointed. Election night he announced that his volunteer Forward Thrust group was disbanding and any future rail transit efforts would be the task of some new organization "with new people and at a new time."[5]

Even decades later, still overflowing with energy and toting around his trademark worn leather briefcase, Ellis would speak wistfully about what could have been if that Atlanta money had stayed in Seattle where it belonged. "What could have been" were words that haunted train transit supporters for the next 25 years.

Following the failed vote, the recession continued eating away at the region. With the mood so gloomy two real-estate agents put up a billboard at a busy street near Sea-Tac International Airport: "Will the last person leaving SEATTLE—Turn out the lights!" The two realtors considered it a lighthearted response to the pervasive pessimism, certainly unaware that the billboard would become a cultural milepost symbolizing this era in the city's history.

As if to make up for the mass transit failures, voters in 1972 approved a sales tax increase for a countywide all-bus system called Metro Transit. People settling into the farthest corners of King County meant that traffic congestion was no longer just a downtown problem. From its birth in 1972, Metro would grow into the tenth-largest transit bus agency in the nation, eventually carrying an average of around 400,000 passengers each weekday.

Despite Metro's success with buses, a transit vacuum remained in Central Puget Sound. The idea of a modern light rail system that would connect the region remained shoved off into the corner.

• • •

Greg Nickels, former Seattle mayor and Sound Transit Board chair, said when you study the history of mass transit in the Puget Sound region, "it's either ascending or it's road kill." After the 1968 and 1970 failed elections, it was road kill.

The idea of a modern rail system that would whisk people congestion-free to their jobs or schools and stores lay dormant for a decade until the early 1980s, when Metro and a regional planning body called the Puget Sound Council of Governments undertook a series of feasibility studies. In the great tradition of Seattle government, studies begat more studies until their offspring filled research libraries across the region.

Energetic and brimming with optimism, Nickels began working in local politics when he was 19 years old. He was elected to the King County Council in 1987 and one of his main platforms was resurrecting the idea of mass transit for the Seattle region. In 1988, two decades after the first failed Forward Thrust ballot, he and fellow councilmember Cynthia Sullivan, who herself would later become a Sound Transit Board member, sponsored a King County advisory ballot to break the stalemate over what Nickels would later say was "the ability to use light *and* rail in the same sentence."

The advisory ballot was just that: advisory. Unburdened by commitments or taxes, the ballot did however test the idea of accelerating light rail planning and 70 percent of voters said yes. If nothing else, that 70 percent gave the notion credibility and now the conversation about light *and* rail began again in earnest.

Rob McKenna, a rail opponent who was a King County Council member and Sound Transit Board member, pointed out that the advisory ballot had no hard cost or ridership estimates and, he said, it allowed backers to say its passage proved the popularity of rail. "It had the effect of rigging all the analysis and skewing it towards the conclusion that we had to have light rail," McKenna would later say.[6]

Nonetheless, a small planning team was formed and, in the tradition of uninspired government titles, called itself the High-Capacity Transit Team. They were mostly Metro employees on loan to the project and tucked away on the 15th floor of Metro's 1930 art deco Exchange Building in downtown Seattle. In the early 1990s, the team began providing the building blocks for light rail. Their work seemed to attract smart, talented people who would eventually shape the culture and lay the groundwork for Sound Transit. Bob White, the future Sound Transit executive director, and Paul Matsuoka, who would become his deputy, were both on the Metro planning team.

Meanwhile 60 miles south in Olympia rumblings about mass transit for the Seattle area began bubbling out of offices and hallways and onto the floor of the Washington State Legislature. Ruth Fisher, a longtime Tacoma lawmaker and tireless chair of the Senate Transportation Committee, was brewing up a bill to bring mass transit to Central Puget Sound—basically from Everett in the north to Tacoma in the south, and from Seattle east across Lake Washington to Bellevue. That bill, aided by her relentless force of personality, was approved in the 1992 legislative session and rolled out to the waiting arms of transit believers in King, Snohomish, and Pierce counties.

At the same time a new generation of leaders was taking stock of mass transit. The election of 1992 was particular meaningful for Snohomish County where future Sound Transit Board members Dave Earling and Bob Drewel were first taking office.

Earling grew up in Spokane and earned a music performance degree from Washington State University before moving to the Puget Sound region, where he became a community college music teacher and band director. Later, though he would continue to play taps every Memorial Day at the Edmonds Memorial Cemetery, he gave up teaching to become the owner of Edmonds Realty. He was a smart and able businessman whose interest in civic activities and transportation brought him to the Edmonds City Council and then the board overseeing the regional transit issue. Eventually he would become mayor of Edmonds. He had a quick wit and ready smile but his probing questions made clear that he wasn't some small town council member about to be rolled by the big city politicians downtown.

Also in 1992 Bob Drewel was elected Snohomish County Executive. The former president of Everett Community College was as comfortable on the back of a horse in an Everett Fourth of July parade as he was in a Boeing Company boardroom. One of his first hires was Joni Earl, the city manager of Mill Creek. Earl had impressed Drewel with her work with cities, as well as with United Way and other charitable organizations. Drewel was a guest at her wedding to Charlie Earl, head of the Snohomish County Public Utility District. Earl joined Drewel's management team as deputy county executive. They were a perfect complement to each other's strengths. Where he was the big picture visionary, she brought an accountant's detailed attention to the day-to-day operation of more than 2,000 county employees. The Puget Sound region would eventually learn that Joni Earl, the Bremerton-born, WSU-educated executive, was much more than anyone's deputy.

Although Drewel was proving adept at politics and building consensus, he admittedly knew little about transportation.

"When I first came into office I asked Joni does this mean I have to do this transportation stuff? She said no it means *we* have to do this transportation stuff and I said that's fair enough."[7]

• • •

Snohomish County, located just north of Seattle, was never a regional transportation player, but Drewel quickly became a believer. He and Earl went to work. If building mass transit was actually going to happen, Drewel figured the urban areas outside Seattle could ill afford to be left out. In fact, the City of Everett would eventually file a lawsuit against mass transit not because of the cost but because city and business leaders didn't think rail would reach Everett fast enough.

The transit vacuum created from the failure to approve a mass transit system decades earlier was becoming painfully obvious in everyday commutes. As the region's population and job creation grew, so did congestion. Between 1970 and 1994, traffic volumes rose 180 percent at the Swamp Creek freeway interchange in Lynnwood, 178 percent near Southcenter, and 232 percent near the Interstate 90 interchange with Interstate 405.

Between 1960 and 1990 the number of jobs in Central Puget Sound more than doubled, while the population grew 82 percent and the region was now home to more than two million people. Adding to the traffic problem, the number of registered vehicles had increased faster than the population. By 1991, there was nearly one registered vehicle for every man, woman, and child in the area. People in all those vehicles were driving more and longer distances. The state Department of Transportation found that vehicle miles traveled increased by 84 percent between 1981 and 1991—from 30 million to 55.2 million.[8]

As the morning and afternoon rush hour became rush *hours*, "something has to be done" was the often-muttered refrain.

From his office in Everett, Drewel fought to keep the rail planning effort from becoming what he called a Seattle inside game. He knew the leaders outside the Seattle core in Pierce and Snohomish counties could not walk away from serious attempts to build a regional mass transit system. "There was a strong feeling if you blew this one you're not going to get another bite of the apple," he said.

Ruth Fisher's mass transit bill was truly regional. It required that the county councils in King, Pierce, and Snohomish counties vote to create the Regional Transit Authority, not a foregone conclusion given the diverse outlooks on those councils and the hesitation about spending taxpayer transportation dollars for anything other than roads and bridges. When the three councils eventually approved the new agency, the RTA was up and running. Mass transit, still an obscure notion in the minds of most people, was now at least invited into the discussion.

Early on, the rail planning project, led by David Kalberer with Bob White as his deputy, had an annual budget of $11 million. The tiny RTA staff was overworked, but there was strong camaraderie and a sense of mission.

Many who joined early stayed on. When Ron Endlich began managing efforts to plan and bring light rail from downtown Seattle to Northgate, his two daughters were in diapers. He would still be at Sound Transit managing that north corridor when his daughters were out of college.

Tim Healy, who would become the agency's marketing director, stepped straight from a Seattle University classroom into a job writing copy for Metro, which at the time was building a bus tunnel under downtown Seattle. City leaders had enough foresight to design the bus tunnel with the correct turning radius and size to one day handle light rail. In 1990 when the tunnel was finished, Healy had the choice of working on the new regional rail plan or writing about natural gas buses. He chose natural gas buses—until he sat through his first meeting. He quickly switched to rail and would remain at Sound Transit for decades.

Similar was David Beal, who was born and raised in Chicago and working there on commuter rail and planning analysis. Recently married, Beal and his wife talked about moving away from the Windy City. But where to go? He'd met and enjoyed RTA staff at national rail conferences and although he'd never been, "I'd heard that Seattle was supposed to be cool."[9] Soon thereafter, he joined the fledgling rail planning effort in Seattle and stayed the next 25 years.

The inaugural RTA board meeting in Bellevue in September 1993 drew scant interest from the public and the press, meriting only a brief story buried deep inside the *Seattle Times*. Of more interest that September was the opening of the new I-90 floating bridge over Lake Washington, connecting Seattle to Mercer Island and Bellevue. That same bridge would later be outfitted with tracks to carry Link light rail trains, but that would be over two decades into the future.

Although the RTA was at first largely ignored, insiders like Greg Nickels were on board from the beginning helping set policy and overseeing staff. "We were just starting completely from scratch," he said. "It was bare bones. We had to figure everything out, how to cash checks, everything."

Tom Matoff, the former general manager of Sacramento Regional Transit, was hired as executive director. Before the RTA, as one of the earlier planning efforts, the Joint Regional Policy Committee completed a study for a 20-year, $15 billion regional rail transit project. The plan was criticized for being too pricy. One of those early critics was Matoff, who believed that instead of expensive stations and trains using tracks fully separated from cars and trucks, the region should build a system where trains would run, like streetcars, in mixed traffic.

As future director White would recall, when Matoff came to Seattle "he kind of put [the cost estimating consultants] off to the side and his group changed the product and changed the numbers and I think some harm was done to the numbers at that point frankly."[10]

While the RTA staff continued its number-crunching and feasibility work on the 15th floor of the Exchange Building, business and community leaders fanned out to drum up support and help shape a package that would be palatable to taxpayers in the new RTA district. The district itself would be vast and diverse, some 1,080 square miles and containing about 40 percent of the entire state's population.

Mike Vaska was a young attorney at the downtown Seattle law firm of Foster Pepper. He grew up in Seattle, attended Stanford University, then law school in Chicago, and now was back home looking to get involved in his home town. That involvement would include joining the Greater Seattle Chamber of Commerce. "Someone said there's this light rail thing it's going to take a while, might take two or three years," he recalled. Because none of the chamber's senior members wanted any part of the light rail effort, they sent Vaska. "So I'm the junior guy on this Seattle Chamber committee and I don't know anyone or anything about anything, basically fell off the turnip truck." He would become one of the earliest and most committed leaders fighting for mass transit in the region.

All the early effort and planning came together on October 29, 1994, when the RTA Board agreed to send a 16-year, $6.7 billion high-capacity transit proposal to voters in a special election scheduled for March 1995. The enabling legislation written by Fisher required that the transit plan come to voters within two years of the RTA's creation. Waiting until the fall when voter turnout would be better would have been too late. So March it was, some four months hence, and full speed ahead.

Internally there was anything but unanimity about the plan. Two RTA Board members voted against putting it on the ballot. Ed Hansen, the mayor of Everett, said it was unfair because it didn't have enough for Everett, most conspicuously no light rail. The city eventually filed suit against the RTA and unsuccessfully sought state legislation that would allow it to withdraw from the transit district.

Also voting no was board member Jane Hague, who was on the King County Council representing cities east of Seattle across Lake Washington. Business leaders on the Eastside, including Kemper Freeman Jr., the powerful Bellevue real estate developer and high-end shopping mall owner, vehemently opposed rail transit. Freeman was smart, well connected, politically savvy and had lots of money—so much money he was willing to part with huge chunks of it to stop train transit. He once spent $1.1 million from his own pockets on a failed attempt to ban light rail from the I-90 bridge into the Eastside.[11]

Few argued the importance of transportation. The argument, simply put, was how to spend the majority of public tax dollars: on roads or on transit. Mass transit advocates saw trains as opportunity. They would connect diverse populations to the world-class education at the University of Washington, or to jobs, shopping, and community services. "To me, there's a kind of race and social justice aspect to it to be able to provide that access to the people who will benefit most from it," Nickels said.

Freeman argued the automobile, not rail transit, exemplifies freedom and mobility. Over the decades his fight against Sound Transit would cost him enough to buy a fleet of luxury automobiles.

But even some on the inside were skeptical of this mass transit plan. Vaska sought counsel from Dan Evans, the widely admired former Washington governor and U.S. senator, who had an office in Vaska's law firm. "I said to Dan I don't think this passes, it's too big, not the right balance and I don't know what to do. Do I support or not support it?"

The former Republican governor gave Vaska advice that he would never forget. He told the young attorney that no piece of legislation is perfect but if you really believe in the cause, even if you don't think it will pass, support it and you'll be in the center of re-shaping it. "I said ok and threw myself all in on trying to pass something I didn't think would pass," Vaska recalled.

• • •

Election Day 1995.

Dark clouds from the failed 1968 and 1970 Forward Thrust ballot measures once again seemed to hang ominously over light rail. Just before the vote Boeing, still the region's largest employer, announced layoffs of more than 6,700 employees.

So it was no surprise that in March 1995, the first child of the failed Forward Thrust would suffer the same fate. Voters again turned back rail, this time with 53.5 percent saying no.

The measure was particularly toxic in Everett, where nearly eight of every 10 voters rejected it. "We were so unpopular in Everett, prohibition would have polled better," Nickels said.

Aubrey Davis, the former regional administrator for the Urban Mass Transportation Administration who lived on Mercer Island across Lake Washington from Seattle, wasn't surprised it went down. "I thought they had too many baubles on their tree," he said.[12]

The next day supporters began their autopsy, wondering if after three failures in three decades light rail in Central Puget Sound was permanent roadkill. At a post-election board meeting, leaders of the pro-RTA campaign testified they believed the rejected plan was too big, too expensive, would take too long to build, and was too complicated to explain.

Other than that, apparently, it was perfect.

There was a new sense of urgency among the rail crowd that if they were to try again with voters, this time it had to be right. Ruth Fisher's legislation stated that if a measure failed at the ballot box a second time, the agency would be dissolved.

But how much enthusiasm and money could you squeeze out of supporters and donors for another full-blown ballot run? Clearly, the plan needed significant alteration to make it passable or the dream of bringing modern mass transit to Central Puget Sound would be wasted for another generation.

Vaska recalled the view at the time was "we've tried this before with Jim Ellis and we didn't get the vote then, didn't get the vote in '95, this is just not going to happen, the politics are just too tough."

Again, Vaska sought out former Gov. Dan Evans. "He would say you know this rail transit thing is the hardest thing this region has ever tried to do because of the geography and because of the politics. My friend Jim Ellis couldn't get it done, so don't be discouraged if you have setbacks because it's really hard."

Supporters knew all about setbacks—what they desperately needed was a win.

Vaska didn't believe rail technology was the problem with the first plan; it was the size of the package and the strong feeling outside Seattle that it would only benefit the region's largest city. He believed suburban voters were thinking "it'll never get out to where we live, we'll get screwed again."

So it was back to the drawing board one last time. The second and last possible child of Forward Thrust was on its way.

• • •

Bob Watt was in his first week as CEO of the influential Greater Seattle Chamber of Commerce when Mike Vaska swept into his office.

Vaska, chair of the Chamber Transportation Committee, said "Ok the [RTA] measure got defeated two weeks ago, what are you going to do to pass it?"

Watt thought for a second: "well that sounds like a good challenge."[13] Watt had been Deputy Mayor to former Seattle Mayor Norm Rice so he knew the players and the politics in Central Puget Sound. His first call was to Bob Gogerty, a longtime political strategist and behind-the-scenes power broker for left-leaning causes. If anyone needed to get involved it was Gogerty, whose first political job was on the 1968 Forward Thrust campaign.[14]

Soon after that phone call, a series of focus groups were organized across Puget Sound.

Watt recalled how the focus groups began by asking participants if they thought the Seattle area should have a light rail system. Generally, 10 of 10 hands went up. Participants were then taken through the grainy details of the mass transit proposal. Now, they were asked, how many would move forward with light rail? Maybe three hands would inch up. To Watt, it was clear that once you dove from a 10,000-foot overview into the tangled details below, everybody suddenly became a transit planner. They'd criticize the plan for being too close to their house or too far from their work or too big or too small. Finally, in desperation one night, participants were simply asked if the region ought to just get started? Nine or 10 hands shot back up.

And that, Watt said, became the essence of the second campaign. Damn the details, just get started.

An intense public outreach effort was launched with the support and involvement of business leaders, to develop a plan that better fit the temperament and pocketbook of the region. A sounding board of prominent citizens included Jim Ellis, the father of Forward Thrust, who remained active in Seattle-area causes.

At the same time the Seattle Chamber led a serious effort to engage and persuade Eastside business and civic leaders, including longtime critic Kemper Freeman, to recognize the need for rail transit.

"The sessions were run carefully enough that I think everyone in the room, even probably including Kemper, felt it was a serious attempt to listen and understand concerns and try to find common ground and therefore it neutralized a lot of people and in fact it caused some people on the Eastside to become supporters," Watt said. But Freeman not only said no, he said "hell no" and spent the next two decades fighting light rail.

Bob Drewel agreed to chair the RTA Board. Drewel had a talent for bringing diverse thinkers together. He also represented a clean break, having no ties to the earlier mass transit studies.

"As badly as we did in Everett, it was pretty gutsy I thought (for Drewel) to step up and be willing to take the reins of this thing," Nickels said.

Inside the RTA change happened fast. Director Matoff quickly terminated all consulting contracts and reduced agency spending by 60 percent. Kathryn DeMeritt, who joined the RTA as a graphic designer in 1994, remembers when one day an "axe man" suddenly appeared in the office. He wasn't there to chop wood. "His job was to figure out who should go and who should stay," she said. "That did not help morale at all."[15] Before long the staff of nearly 150, including consultants, numbered just 23.

Two months after the failed vote Matoff resigned. Bob White, who in the first campaign had successfully led a demonstration project that ran commuter trains from Everett and Tacoma into Seattle, was given the reins and a hearty good luck.

The true believers who remained were asked to help out by cobbling together jobs they scarcely knew. That was how David Beal, fresh from Chicago, became acting finance director. "I only know a little bit about finance but that was how thin we were," he said. "We paid a few bills and we paid salaries, there wasn't much high finance going on." Beal and his wife were considering bidding on a house, but with mass transit facing such an uncertain future, he wondered if it was a good idea.

White, the new director, recalled that there was now only one engineer on staff. White himself was the only project manager left and his strength was commuter rail, not light rail or express buses.

Meanwhile, as the agency shrank to nearly nothing, a listening tour of board members and RTA supporters worked its way around Central Puget Sound from Everett to Tacoma to Bellevue. Over and over, people outside Seattle said they were worried that the big city would suck up all the money, leaving everyone else fighting for loose change. From that concern came "subarea equity." The region was split into five geographic subareas. Subarea equity promised that dollars raised in a subarea would only go to train or bus projects benefiting that subarea.

"I thought it was a terrible policy but a necessary political compromise," Nickels said. He said it was regressive in that financially healthy subareas, like East King County, couldn't use that financial strength anywhere else in the region but East King County. At the time it seemed more like balkanized states than a unified country.

As they toured around, board members heard similar comments: make it smaller, make sure it connects with other transit, and for god's sake make sure our tax dollars aren't building tunnels in Seattle.

The new plan was forged in compromise and included direct involvement from the chamber and the business community on size, scope, and cost. Under the new blueprint, called Sound Move, light rail would be built in phases, the first phase connecting the airport with downtown Seattle and the University of Washington. The plan would include a network of express bus routes connecting major cities in the region, commuter rail running on BNSF Railway Company tracks from Everett and Tacoma into Seattle, and improvements to the state highway high-occupancy-vehicle network. There would be subarea equity and, in what would later prove impossible, the entire package was promised to be finished in just 10 years. The plan was $3.9 billion, with a 0.4 percent increase in sales tax and 0.3 percent increase in the Motor Vehicle Excise Tax for those living in the RTA district. The proposal was six years shorter and 40 percent cheaper than the first ballot measure.

Watt took the second set of plans out to Phil Condit, Boeing's new CEO. Condit, who started out as an aerodynamics engineer and worked his way up, was soon on his hands and knees poring over the plans spread out on his office floor. The Boeing CEO liked what he saw. He not only became personally involved, he convened a top-level business fundraising effort and agreed to be an honorary co-chair. Boeing issued a statement saying that "it is impossible to run an efficient company when your workers are stuck on the commute to work." Microsoft also joined as a major campaign contributor.

The measure was scheduled for the November 5, 1996, general ballot, allowing five months for the campaign.

The RTA backers made it a high-visibility, high-energy campaign with TV and newspaper ads, along with grassroots volunteer phone banks and sign waving at sporting events. Besides corporate donors, medium and small contributions flowed in until the campaign eventually had more than a million dollars.

Opponents, again centered in East King County, argued that light rail wouldn't meet the needs of most commuters who neither lived nor worked in the urban centers served by rail. The Vote No crowd raised several hundred thousand dollars from trucking, road builders, home builders, and Bellevue retail and real estate interests. Kemper Freeman, whose disdain for the agency was evident, crossed the region debating RTA backers at chamber breakfasts, Rotary luncheons, and evening community forums.

At the Downtown Bellevue Association, a group inclined to agree with him, Freeman announced that: "the RTA sucks." And then on a conservative radio talk show, he said the plan had no chance of passing.[16]

The opponents were united in their contempt for the RTA plan. Beyond that, however, there was little agreement on how to solve the region's growing traffic congestion. Freeman wanted freeway improvements to carry more cars. Another group wanted to extend the mile-long Monorail built for the 1962 World's Fair, others wanted expanded freeway HOV lanes or free buses. Emory Bundy, an environmentalist turned light rail critic, believed the region should save its transit dollars until a new technology emerged, whatever and whenever that would be.

Tim Healy and graphic designer Kathryn DeMeritt were at the Shoreline Park-and-Ride lot waving campaign signs on their off hours when somebody recognized them as RTA employees and claimed, loudly, that they only cared because their jobs were at stake. "I said I like to think that if this failed and I lost my job I could get another job," Healy said. "But if this fails twice on the ballot the region is not going to get another chance, it's not coming back a third time."[17]

The month prior to the election all RTA staffers received layoff notices from King County. If the election failed, they would indeed all be out of a job.

• • •

Election day, Tuesday, November 5, 1996.

The Seattle area had grown up since 1968, developing a newfound confidence and the personality of a big city. There was more economic diversity and the soil was fertile for startups that would eventually grow into the huge multinational giants of Amazon and Starbucks. Boeing and Microsoft were hiring and young people moving in brought with them a new energy and sense of possibility. Even the Seattle Mariners baseball team a year earlier had shaken off its woebegone history to make an improbable run to the playoffs. Future Hall of Famer Ken Griffey Jr., who wore his hat backwards and embodied the youthful vibrancy of the city, was the hottest star in the major leagues.

Instead of looking back at what was, the region seemed determined to explore what could be. Even the curmudgeonly *Seattle Times* editorial board urged voters to approve the mass transit plan.

When Healy pulled up to the RTA's campaign headquarters on election night he heard cheers rocking the building. The early returns had started coming in and a feeling of disbelief and then elation swept the room. As the evening wore on it became even clearer that, shockingly, unbelievably, light rail was coming to Central Puget Sound. The second child of Forward Thrust lived.

The Sound Move plan passed 56.5 percent region-wide, an amazing feat given the earlier failed efforts. Snohomish County voters approved the plan by 55 percent, it won in Pierce County, and by an overwhelming 70 percent in Seattle. The measure even won by 54 percent in Bellevue, home to Kemper Freeman. Historically, it was the largest transportation tax and public works project ever approved in the state.

Healy remembers thanking Bob White's wife, Katherine Rice, for keeping her husband sane through the two elections. "I really attribute it to him, his leadership at the time because he was able to soothe all the board's misgivings about the first election," Healy said.

The next morning Seattle residents opened their *Seattle Times* to a picture of Healy wrapped up in a giant bear hug from fellow RTA staffer Johnathan Jackson.

Even in an election that gave Bill Clinton a second term in Washington, D.C., and sent former Sound Transit Board Member Gary Locke to the governor's mansion in Olympia, the *Seattle Times* editorial board found time to take note of the regional transit vote: "The impressive victory of the three-county regional transit plan spoke directly to the voters' willingness to embrace and pay for government-provided services deemed worthwhile. Unsnarling traffic seemed an entirely appropriate function for government."[18]

Elsewhere, the newspaper quoted board member Dave Earling, who said that in recent weeks people began to understand "that this was their last shot for quite a while."

Brett Bader, campaign consultant to the RTA opponents, attributed some of the victory margin to the heavy Democratic voter turnout. He noted that the opposition was outspent about 4-to-1. But Bob Gogerty, the RTA's campaign guru, said the vote showed people will vote to tax themselves "if the campaign is honest about its good and bad points."[19]

The election, Sound Transit's Healy would succinctly conclude, was "one of those weird miracle things."

But little did any of the people at that victory celebration know, the real battle for light rail had just begun.

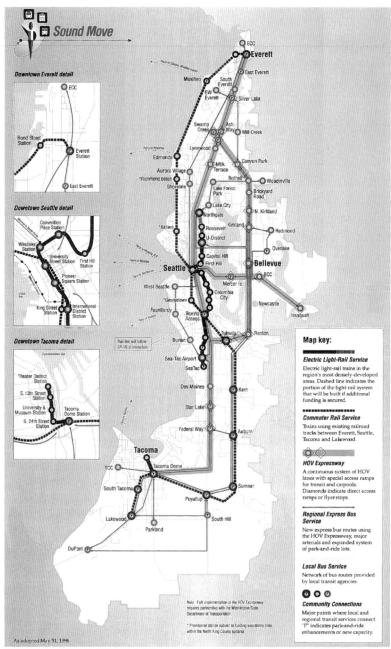

The original map showing the Sound Transit system of trains and buses, as adopted by the Board of Directors in 1996. *Courtesy Sound Transit.*

2

Don't Screw Up

Go forward. Do good. Don't screw up.
—Bob White

Reality never took a day off. Any lingering exhilaration from election night was quickly swept aside by the task ahead. And it was daunting—a completely new agency building a light rail line over challenging terrain in a region that had never before had one. The fledgling agency was also tasked with setting up a network of regional express buses and then begin running commuter trains on BNSF Railway Company freight tracks. And oh, by the way, all those services and equipment had to be planned, negotiated, bought, built, and running in 10 years.

Soon after the election the 23 RTA employees, still a little shell-shocked by the election results, understood that besides building a transit system they were also building a bureaucracy. But here was a once-in-a-generation chance to assemble a different kind of bureaucracy and in doing so become innovators in the glacial-speed world of government. The new agency would have a performance management system patterned after private industry along with generous health and retirement benefits to attract talent.

So far so good, but what next?

Paul Matsuoka, who held a master's degree in urban planning from UCLA and would later become deputy director of Sound Transit, said the RTA felt like a startup company. Noticeably lacking though was the practical experience in how to start a startup. "We were like let's go hire people. How do we advertise? Do we advertise in the *Seattle Times* and if we do that will the *Everett Herald* be mad? We had no policy guidelines, no HR [human resources department] to turn to. We were like throwing tracks out in front of a runaway locomotive."[1]

The fledgling agency was still working in Metro offices in downtown Seattle, sitting at Metro desks, using Metro computers, Metro pens and Metro paper clips. Shortly after the November election, Metro congratulated the 23 and then told them to be gone by January.

"It was overwhelming at times," said Matsuoka, who routinely worked 15-hour days. "I was in charge of personnel, affirmative action, government relations, communications and marketing. We were holding it all together."

Soon after the election Tim Healy was at a marketing conference in Reno, Nevada, telling other transit agencies how the RTA successfully sold its plan to voters. It was the early days of email and he remembers receiving a message from the home office in Seattle. The email included pictures of various office chairs. Healy shook his head and turned to a colleague also at the conference. With so much important work squeezed into such a short time frame, "I can't believe we're voting on office chairs." But building a $3.9 billion mass transit system also meant building an office and an office needed chairs.

It wasn't long before the RTA moved out of Metro into another temporary home, this one an old five-story bank building on Second and Spring Streets in downtown Seattle. Here, finally out of the giant shadow of Metro, most staffers found the work endless but exciting, starting with finding a decent name.

The name RTA screamed government acronym. The feeling was that the new bus and train services needed snappy names that would make sense to the public and invoke positive feelings. Short of that, the names at least couldn't be fodder for derision, such as when someone pointed out that said aloud, the acronym for the Citizen Oversight Committee was COC. The name was changed to Citizen Oversight Panel.

As for a name of the agency itself, marketing consultants hired by the RTA researched and then pondered, and then pondered some more, sifting through a mediocre assortment of labels, hoping they'd eventually land on something spectacular. Additional suggestions were made by local newspapers and listeners to a Seattle radio talk show. After reviewing more than 50 names, the RTA, as if in desperation, finally agreed to call it Sound Transit. For the associated pieces of the system, consultants pushed Northwest-themes like Chinook and Eagle but the RTA Board eventually approved Sounder commuter rail, Link light rail, and ST Express buses.

• • •

The plan at first was to run the entire operation with around 100 full-time employees. Those 100 inspired employees, it was thought, would be enough to manage the fleet of consultants hired to do everything else. Brian McCartan, who joined the agency as deputy finance director and would later become finance director, said there was no understanding of what kind of organization it would take to negotiate for property, secure permits, dig tunnels, lay tracks, build stations and park-and-ride lots, and then actually run those buses and trains.[2]

Predictably, the 100-employee idea was scrapped early on and the hiring binge began. Between 1997 and 2000, about 120 new, full-time employees joined Sound Transit. The bank building overflowed with new hires and consultants, many from cities around the nation with expertise in light rail engineering or systems engineering or procurement or planning tunnels. So many employees were brought on so quickly there wasn't room for everyone. New staffers found themselves squeezed into out-of-the-way conference rooms where they tried to work quietly while meetings droned on just a few feet away.

Henry Cody joined on as a deputy construction manager for light rail. He'd spent 17 years with Metro in wastewater treatment plants and construction of the Downtown Seattle Transit Tunnel. His first office at Sound Transit was a desk in a supply closet. The gregarious Cody made the best of it: "It was a great place to sit because when people came in for paper and pencils I got to meet everyone."[3]

Cody remembers leaving his supply closet for department meetings on light rail. "We had all these people from all over the country and everybody was from a different state and everybody was trying to do it their way," he said. "Everybody kept saying this is the way we're going to do it because this is the way we did it in Utah and we kept saying 'but this is Seattle.'"

The agency settled on a unique organizational structure that involved three "lines of business," or LOBs as the inevitable acronym became, with each LOB operating as its own mini-Sound Transit. Leading all three lines was Bob White with Paul Matsuoka as his deputy.

One LOB would plan, start, and manage the ST Express bus program. The idea was that Sound Transit would buy the buses and pay for their upkeep while contracting with King County Metro, Pierce Transit, and Community Transit in Snohomish County for maintenance and drivers.

Those agencies already had maintenance yards and infrastructure in place so Sound Transit could roll out its new routes as soon as the buses were ordered, built, and delivered, which took about two years. While those other transit agencies already ran mostly shorter local routes, Sound Transit would concentrate on the long-haul commuter routes from outlying cities into Seattle and back.

The second line of business was Sounder commuter trains that would run on freight tracks from Everett in the north and Tacoma in the south into King Street Station in Seattle. Trains would run weekdays during peak commute hours into Seattle in the morning and back out to Everett and Tacoma in the evening. The new agency would own the train cars and locomotives and planned to lease time on the tracks from BNSF, a negotiating experience that would test the stamina of everyone involved. Amtrak was under contract to maintain the trains at its yard in the industrial area south of downtown Seattle.

The third LOB was Link light rail. For this most expensive and visible piece of the puzzle, the plan was to hire and oversee contractors to build the tracks and stations. A 1.6-mile streetcar line in Tacoma, called Tacoma Link, would be built and run by Sound Transit.

With its basic organizational structure in place, Sound Transit hired its first directors in 1997. Desmond Brown, who grew up on an Arkansas dairy farm before earning a law degree with honors from Harvard, was chief counsel. When he was young, Brown was given the option of filling his days studying or milking cows. He chose books. In an agency filled with smart people, Brown's intellect stood out.

Agnes Govern, the new director of ST Express, had been assistant general manager of the Snohomish County Public Utility District and had held various management positions at Metro. Before long she was one of the go-to directors in the building. One of her top managers once had WWAD (What Would Agnes Do) stitched on the back of his Sound Transit baseball cap.

Paul Price had been Coaster commuter rail director in San Diego and in just three years would have commuter trains running between Tacoma and Seattle.

Paul Bay, a longtime light rail manager with nine children and a degree in civil engineering from Stanford, signed on as Link light rail director. Bay had more than 35 years of experience, including light rail planning and design in Minneapolis, Salt Lake City, San Diego, Portland, Denver, and Orlando.

In his hiring announcement, Bay used the Chinese philosopher Lao Tzu to describe his leadership philosophy: "A leader is not so great when people say, 'See what he has done.' A leader is greatest when the people say, 'See what we have done.'"[4]

Sound Transit's organizational structure was designed to give its directors a laser-beam focus on their line of business, which made sense in theory. In practice, the structure created three silos with limited cross-department functions. A talented project manager in Sounder, for example, could not be used to solve a problem in Link.

What the young agency lacked in experience and structure it tried to make up for with hard work. "We'd just sit down, talk about it and you do this, you do this and boom we'd go," said Brown. "I was working six and seven days a week and a lot of other people were too. I was having fun. It was pretty cool."[5]

• • •

From the very beginning, there was a cornerstone commitment that the agency deliver what it promised voters within the 10-year time frame. "If that's your mandate, you're going to figure out a way to do it," Finance Director McCartan said. "It was defeatism to come to Bob (White) and say early on that there's high risk and we should tell the board. Every natural instinct was to say how can we do this? Let's start thinking optimistically."

That sense of urgency was there from the beginning. On election night, when it became apparent that the new mass transit system would win approval, White reminded staff not to think of it as a 10-year project, but rather a project of 120 months. Because, he told his troops, every minute, every day, every month counts.

Agnes Govern said in an ideal world everyone would understand that it takes at least a year to get your internal processes together and really know how you're going to deliver those new services. "We didn't have that luxury. Bob (White) would say it again and again: 'we are building the bicycle as we are riding it.' There's no way you can ride the bicycle as you build it and be at all graceful about it. You're going to make mistakes."[6]

Govern remembers feeling fortunate that her ST Express bus department was comparatively low profile. Sounder commuter rail and Link light rail were glitzy and new and that was where the public's attention focused. "We just kind of kept our head down, so the mistakes we made were under the radar," she said.

Despite the low profile, ST Express buses quickly became the agency's workhorse. Buses began running in late 1999 and in the first full year carried more than four million riders.

As those 120 months began to fly by, the agency and its board felt the vice-tightening pressure to deliver tangible successes that they could point to with press releases and groundbreaking ceremonies.

So, in the beginning, small successes were pumped into full-scale events. First up was groundbreaking for the Ash Way bus park-and-ride lot near Lynnwood in Snohomish County. The night before Tim Healy, the agency's marketer, spray-painted hardware store shovels gold so they could be used for the ceremonial and obligatory first turning of dirt. The media was invited and Sound Transit Board members and local dignitaries made speeches. Not mentioned in the ceremony or press packet was that part of the site was once a former drug house and there were worries, albeit remote, about someone accidentally stepping on a needle.

Not long after came a ceremony at the Tacoma Dome where the first ST Express buses were taking over a Pierce Transit route into Seattle and back. The tagline for the kickoff event was "The Wheels are in Motion" and caps with the tagline were distributed to everyone who attended. One morning about a year later on his way into work, Healy noticed a homeless man in Seattle's Pioneer Square district pushing a shopping cart with all his belongings. The man was wearing a "The Wheels are in Motion" cap. Healy hoped it wasn't a sign of where the agency was headed.

In June 1998 the Sound Transit Board announced that the agency's permanent headquarters would be at the long abandoned Union Station at the south end of downtown near the Kingdome, International District, and Pioneer Square. Under the deal, Sound Transit would pay up to $21 million to renovate the 1911 Beaux-Arts-style building before buying it for one dollar. Renovation of the three-story station began. Scaffolding erected around the building was cocooned inside nearly three acres of plastic to keep dust and debris from drifting onto the street. Ancient wiring and phone lines were replaced with 16 miles of communications and power conduit and over two miles of new piping and ductwork was needed to turn the building into a modern office. Still, Union Station was in surprisingly good shape for having sat vacant for 25 years. The building's showcase public entryway was the Great Hall; its high arching half-moon window, detailed original lights, and the intricate tiled floor were painstakingly restored.[7]

The Great Hall would soon become a favorite setting for high school proms, wedding receptions, movie productions (including the opening scenes from Amazon's *The Man in the High Castle*), and refuge for street dwellers seeking respite from the rain.

• • •

There is a misconception from those outside government that public entities, be they cities, universities, or transit agencies, hold hands and walk together down a path of common good. In practice, working out deals and permits between agencies is often divisive and awkward, particularly when there is fundamental disagreement on goals. The City of Tukwila, for example, took Sound Transit to court over its uncompromising insistence on a less effective, and more expensive, light rail route through its city. The University of Washington insisted on costly changes to the underground light rail route to protect sensitive research equipment. The university was worried that vibrations from light rail trains would compromise experiments in its physics labs. Negotiations dragged on for years.

Bob White said that after the vote just about everybody was naïve about the magnitude of what Sound Transit was trying to do. Conceptually people supported it, but once the agency began carrying out the plan, powerful players and local institutions tried to change it to protect turf, avoid impacts, or better meet their narrow needs.

"It was very raw," Govern recalled. "I think in many ways Metro (Transit) was the hardest to deal with because they were the big player and all of a sudden they weren't anymore. They were in terms of customers and everything else but it was very clear where the future was going, so those were very hard relationships to negotiate."

Meanwhile, the clock was ticking with no visible work finished on light rail. Months turned into years and any grace period the agency had received from the public and community leaders was now fading.

• • •

Inside the offices at Union Station warnings began bubbling up to top management. The first reaction was to clamp a lid on the pot and hope it didn't boil over.

Desmond Brown, besides being chief legal counsel, was also head of the real estate department for a short time. One day the real estate property manager arrived at his office with the bombshell that the budget for Link light rail property acquisition was less than half of what was needed.

Similarly about that time, McCartan was at a meeting with top agency officials when the topic turned to real estate needs for building light rail. The real estate manager said the agency would need to purchase something like 300 pieces of various-sized properties to build the first Link segment. The property would be bought at fair market value, but the process of acquiring private property for public projects can be long and contentious. Paul Bay, light rail director, disagreed with the 300 number, saying the estimate was crazy, that the magnitude would be closer to 50.

"I remember thinking I don't know which is right, but one of them is not right," McCartan recalled. Turns out the property needed was closer to 300 than 50.

By now word was leaking out about the costs piling up with the light rail project. The chamber and business leaders began meeting with Greg Nickels and other board members at the offices of Cocker Fennessy, Sound Transit's public affairs consultants located in Pioneer Square, a quick walk from Union Station.

"Every time Bob (White) would solve a problem another one would pop up," Rick Cocker would recall.[8]

Most worrisome was the ever-rising estimate to dig the 4.5-mile-long light rail tunnels (one for northbound, one for southbound trains) under First Hill, Capitol Hill, and the waters of Portage Bay leading to the University of Washington. It was a particularly difficult dig, deep and with soil conditions that could be a problem. The agency had budgeted up to $500 million for the contract to build the tunnel. Word was spreading that the contract numbers would be much, much higher.

To gauge the temperature of city business leaders, Cocker Fennessy conducted several off-the-record interviews finding growing animosity and precious little support for Sound Transit. Some examples:

> "My sense is that Sound Transit is adrift, if not amuck, and potentially in very serious danger…they have squandered and lost all the good will and momentum we worked to achieve during the campaign."

> "The shit has not hit the fan yet."

> "Bob White's style comes across as arrogance."

> "We just need a miracle. I don't see how we can build what we need to build with the money we have."

> "My concern is that the basic business decisions are wrong. Unless you change those there's nothing you can do. You can't put frosting on a turd."[9]

• • •

Sheila Dezarn, one of Sound Transit's original 23 employees, was heading up the team seeking a federal grant for the light rail line. Although she wasn't involved in the tunnel project she, like everyone at the agency, was aware of the importance of the numbers. Simply put, if the tunnel contract bids came in too high, the entire light rail project could tailspin.

It was a beautiful Seattle Sunday afternoon and Dezarn was in her yard working when Paul Matsuoka called. "We have a problem," he told her. "The tunnel bids came in high. Really, really high."[10]

In fact one of the bids was close to $900 million, almost twice what was budgeted. Dezarn felt her stomach churning. This, she knew, could be crippling. The agency would now have to undertake a grim search to find ways to trim tunnel costs back to something closer to the original estimate. If not, who knew where Sound Transit was headed.

As Brian McCartan would say, a lot was accomplished in those early years. The small agency launched bus service, got commuter rail set to go, had a successful bond issue, and got itself organized from scratch.

But all that was all about to be overwhelmed by the sputtering light rail department.

Time to call Joni Earl.

3
Time to Call Joni

If the other team was sending in 12 people, I sent Joni.
—Bob Drewel

Bremerton, Washington, is an hour ferry boat ride across Puget Sound from downtown Seattle, and in many ways the cities are even farther apart. Urban, sophisticated, with money and skyscrapers, Seattle pays little attention to Bremerton, a shipyard town with its own politics and blue collar values. Some winter mornings as the ferries near Bremerton, the fog at Sinclair Inlet seems to swallow up the boats as they disappear inside.

Bremerton in the 1960s and '70s was a city of about 35,000 residents, whose downtown swelled with sailors when battleships and 20-story high aircraft carriers arrived for overhaul in the Bremerton Naval Shipyard. The USS *Missouri*, site of the Japanese surrender signing that ended World War II, sailed into Bremerton in 1955 and remained a waterfront symbol of strength and endurance for the next three decades.

It was in this city, in that era, that Joni Earl grew up, the youngest of three daughters born to Morrie and Mary Ellen Dawkins, the longtime owners of Evergreen Trophies downtown. Bremerton and its proud blue collar ethic was an important influence in those early years, but it was Earl's parents who defined her. Morrie Dawkins was active in civic life, first on the Bremerton Parks Board, then as mayor, and finally on the city council. He taught his three daughters strong values: public service, hard work, honesty, and personal integrity. People need to know that whatever you say they can take to the bank, Earl's father would tell her.

After high school, Earl earned an associate's degree from Olympic Community College in Bremerton before heading across the water and over the Cascade Mountains to Washington State University in Pullman. Money was tight and she got through by typing term papers

and scrounging odd jobs. On breaks, she cobbled together work with
the City of Bremerton and the county auditor's office, saving precious
dollars whenever she could.

Even with that, desperation set in during the last semester of her
senior year at WSU when she found herself drained of money and carrying a full academic load. Following an emergency family meeting, her
grandparents took out a mortgage for $750 which, because they had no
other debt, was a telling show of faith in their granddaughter's future.

When Earl graduated in 1975 with a bachelor's degree in business and her last $120 in the bank, she and her girlfriends piled into
a Datsun B210 and drove 700 miles to Reno, Nevada, for an end-
of-school party. Even with a cheap hotel, her budget was $20 a day,
hardly enough for high roller gambling. Their final night in Reno she
played keno because, as she would later say, it was the slowest way to
lose money. At 11:40 p.m., just minutes before leaving, she won a
$750 jackpot, drove home, repaid her grandparents, and was free and
clear.[1] Helped along by her family and a little Reno luck, Earl was
ready to take on the rest of her life.

Immediately after WSU, short stints in private sector jobs,
including bank teller, taught her two life lessons: one, she intensely
disliked being a bank teller and two, she never again wanted a job
where she hated money. Eventually she would discover that public
agency jobs, by comparison, were endlessly challenging and there she
found her calling. "There was never a day that started and ended the
way I thought it was going to start and end," she would say. Earl also
appreciated that when dealing with taxpayer money the public has a
say in everything and, she would learn in exquisite detail, they were
never shy about letting her know it.

Earl's public career and family-taught values were tested from
the very beginning when she joined the City of Bremerton's Trea-
sury Office as an accountant. She'd been on the job only a short
time when an unexpected death left an opening for assistant city
treasurer. Fresh out of college and with no significant experience on
her resume, Earl nonetheless decided to take the civil service exam
needed for the job. She finished second, an achievement in itself. But
when she used her accountant's eye to analyze her second place test

results, she noticed a scoring error. Shortly thereafter, Joni Earl had a new title: assistant city treasurer.

The excitement of her new job wore off not long afterwards when she found herself entangled in a potentially career-defining controversy. The city was having trouble converting to a new water billing system and couldn't so much as get the bills out. Months went by. When the city finally fixed the problem, the cumulative water bills for some Bremerton residents were enormous. Years later Earl could still vividly recall the jarring slam of the city finance commissioner's door as he rushed out of his office demanding that some of those water bills be waived. A little research told her that those getting special treatment happened to be the family and friends of the commissioner, which was an elected position. Earl refused to waive the bills. Looking back she said it wasn't a profound moment, but it was early in her career and she felt as if she needed to take a stand—regardless of the pressure—because once you give in to something you know is wrong, where do you stop?

Earl went home that night and talked with her parents. They were proud of her for holding her ground, but worried she would lose her job over it. "I said, yeah, but what have you guys taught us your whole life?" A few months later, when the Bremerton finance commissioner was re-elected for another term, Earl resigned.

• • •

Over the years Earl would round out her schooling with an MBA from the University of Puget Sound in Tacoma as well as executive programs at the University of Colorado and Harvard University. But books only went so far. On the job experience, she found, was the best teacher and for that she was a superior student.

As a young manager in hometown Bremerton, Earl joined the Washington City/County Management Association. The more she learned about running cities, the greater her interest grew. When the city manager job opened in Mill Creek, a city of around 10,000 about 20 miles north of Seattle, she applied and was hired. It was in this small Snohomish County community where she would hone the skills needed to deal with the maddening bureaucracy, minor skirmishes, and outsized personalities that plague even the best run governments. She also learned about regional issues and players, including Bob Drewel, who himself had a big, outgoing personality. And it was there she first earned her reputation as a skillful, hardworking manager who knew how to get projects done.

Drewel, eventually her boss as Snohomish County Executive, would come to rely on her. "I've never met anybody who outworked Joni Earl," he would say.

Long before she'd even thought about joining Sound Transit, Earl was familiar with the agency and its major players, albeit from outside looking in. She'd helped draft the Snohomish County piece of the transit package that was approved by voters in 1996. And she staffed a committee of Sound Transit Board members.

By the year 2000, Drewel was nearing the end of his second term and because of term limits was ineligible for re-election. At the time Earl was starting to think seriously of what was next. As she was pondering the possibilities, a phone call from Bob White changed the arc of her life.

"Hey Joni, I need to pick your brain," White said that summer day in 2000. The Sound Transit leader was desperately in need of a chief operating officer, someone who could scrutinize the faltering organization and its structure and thought Earl would know some good candidates. The more he talked about the job and the problems facing the agency, the more intriguing it became.

Earl recalled that when she expressed an interest in the job herself, White exclaimed: "Are you kidding? Bob Drewel would *kill* me!"

Earl quickly reassured him: "There's a long way between Bob Drewel killing you and me getting the job, so let's not worry about that."

There was something about the Sound Transit opening that fascinated Earl and she felt that even though she didn't know transit, she had the organizational background and skills to make a difference. It would, however, require a 30-mile rush-hour commute from Everett into Seattle and back. But improving the way people get around, after all, was what the new agency was supposed to be about. What better way to learn the misery of a Puget Sound commute than to experience it every day?

White agreed to keep her interest under wraps and the hiring process became a minor cloak-and-dagger affair. Her interview was in a downtown Seattle attorney's office so she could slip in and out undetected. Early on, White told her that the contract to dig the train tunnel from downtown Seattle to Capitol Hill and the University of Washington was getting complicated. In fact, she would learn the problems ran deeper than the tunnel. About a year earlier, in 1999, top management at Sound Transit began detecting warning signs with Link's overall budget. Real estate costs were much higher than expected. Pressures from cities to add expensive route changes and mitigation grew in intensity. Staff and administrative costs were growing beyond anything originally envisioned. Waters were becoming treacherous.

In August 2000, following an extensive review of proposals, the contracting team of Modern Transit Constructors was chosen to present a bid to design and build Link's 4.5-mile-long light rail tunnel from downtown under First Hill, Capitol Hill, and the waters of Portage Bay leading to the University of Washington. The tunnel was always Link's weakest link.

"Portage Bay is basically pudding," said Greg Nickels, former Seattle mayor and Sound Transit Board chair. "It's not solid soil, and we're looking to put a tunnel through pudding, a very long, very deep tunnel."

Concern grew into alarm when Modern Transit Constructors' proposal came in at $728 million, or more than $200 million above what the agency had budgeted. "We knew we were in trouble," White said.

White and the Link team hurriedly assembled closed-door meetings with the contractor in an attempt to negotiate the tunnel numbers down. They were so worried that the numbers would spill out into the public and ruin their negotiations that participants were required to sign confidentiality agreements.

Paul Matsuoka remembers meeting with the tunnel contractors. "I said we don't want a gilded project, we want something safe, reliable and affordable, and you've got to value engineer it down or you won't have a project to build." But weeks of intense negotiations only seemed to shave pennies off the bottom line.

Meanwhile the bid amount, as White said, was hardly a secret. The pool of people who knew the number grew bigger and bigger and some suspected that parts of the consulting community, particularly those desperate to make sure they weren't being held responsible for the high cost, were leaking details. So much for those confidentiality agreements. After a few weeks, it was the worst held secret in Seattle. Not everyone knew the exact bid, they just knew it was more than the agency's estimate—a lot more.

During that time the Sound Transit Board was growing anxious as well. Anne Fennessy, Sound Transit's public affairs consultant and former press secretary for Gov. Mike Lowry, remembers the "come to Jesus," meetings in her office with senior Sound Transit staff and unhappy board members who felt they weren't getting the whole story. They were also becoming increasingly angry with White. "There was a sense that something bad was going on," Fennessy said.[2] Her business partner, Rick Cocker, remembers that the meetings were painful. "There was no confidence in staff at all. Sound Transit staff would come in and they had to prove they weren't lying. It was awful."

When White talked to Earl about joining Sound Transit he told her: "You need to know if you take this job I may not be here." In fact, he was fairly certain his days were numbered. During a meeting around that time at Cocker Fennessy offices in Pioneer Square, Seattle Mayor Paul Schell leaned over to White and said: "You know Bob, this is going to cost you your job."

As White later analyzed that moment, he appreciated the mayor's honesty. "It was you know, get ready buddy. At that point I really knew the exit was coming, it was only what was the best timing for the board."

Mike Vaska, who had remained close to White following the 1996 election, observed from the outside looking in that the agency's budget problems were being hung around White's neck and the rope was tightening. "He was executive director and when you're executive director you get credit for the good stuff and blame for the bad stuff whether you deserve it or not, that's how it works and he knew he was going to have to go, so the question was who do you hire that could be your successor?" Vaska believed that if a good strong leader wasn't hired, the future of Sound Transit was in jeopardy and a generation of work bringing light rail to Central Puget Sound would be lost. In private conversations with Vaska, White said he was convinced that Earl was right for Sound Transit.

By now the leaders in the business community, who felt they had stuck their necks out to help Sound Transit win voter approval in 1996, were beyond anxious.

Bob Watt, Seattle Chamber president, shared his concerns with the agency. "I was worried sick," he said. "We had gone way out on a limb for the ballot measure and supported the agency and wanted to see it succeed but people were really starting to get nervous that the whole project could be terminated. There were a lot of Seattle business people whose names were on it, mine included. There were days I was worried the whole thing could crater."

The public affairs firm Cocker Fennessy heard similar worries when they once again surveyed business leaders from across the region. Again, they got an earful:

> "I am very skeptical. I am disappointed. Sound Transit has played hide the ball. Any other organization with these results, heads would have rolled."

> "What's really needed is to move forward, build confidence by getting started and accomplishing something."

> "I hate to say it, but if it were a stock, you'd sell Sound Transit short right now. There are just too many negatives lurking over the horizon."[3]

Into this growing turmoil stepped Joni Earl, who agreed to become Sound Transit's Chief Operating Officer at a starting salary of $140,000 a year. She was 47 years old and in the prime of her career, skilled and confident following years of running the day-to-day operations of Snohomish County government. She was already widely respected in local government and business circles in Snohomish County where she was on the board of directors for a local bank, Everett Schools Foundation, and the United Way campaign cabinet. She was also the first-ever woman to join the Mill Creek Rotary Club. Even so, Sound Transit would test her like nothing before.

Drewel remembers when Earl arrived at his office in September 2000 for their regular Monday morning meeting. Unbeknownst to Drewel, Earl was coming in to announce her resignation.

"I had this little couch by the desk and she came in and sat down and said 'I'm leaving.' I said 'we're just starting,' and she said 'no, I'm leaving' and then she broke into tears and said she had this whole speech prepared. I said, 'Joni, what's going on?' And so she told me and we talked about it and I said, 'Joni, let me tell you, you better be prepared to take that operation over within the next year or so,' because I knew enough about what was going on internally and I knew Bob White just couldn't survive."

4

Train to Nowhere

Bob, you've got a problem.
—Joni Earl

Seattle in 2000—before the explosion of smart phones, social media, and transit blogs—was a two-newspaper town where traditional media reporters and editors set the daily news agenda.

The Seattle-area media employed reporters working full time on the transportation beat and Sound Transit was becoming the biggest and juiciest story in town. The papers in neighborhoods and outlying cities in the district also had reporters carefully watching Sound Transit. Newspaper editorial boards, whose job was to consider and then comment on issues, were also eager to weigh in on anything Sound Transit, particularly its light rail program. Strong editorials not only influenced public opinion, they sometimes prompted lawmakers and government leaders to change direction.

Thomas Shapley, a longtime member of the *Seattle-Post Intelligencer* editorial board, said his newspaper's board supported increased transit but wanted to make sure it was done right and that taxpayer dollars were spent wisely. "The most important thing was that we got transit that was legitimate, economical, successful and did the job," he said.[1]

Whenever a newspaper broke a big story the city's three television stations followed like the tail on a kite. The opposition was always there as well, eager to salt old wounds.

In August of 2000 Emory Bundy, a Seattle environmentalist turned zealous light rail critic, published a story called "Why Rail?" in a Portland, Oregon, magazine called *Open Spaces*. In that article Bundy argued against light rail in favor of a mix of alternatives including more buses, bicycles, carpooling, vanpooling, and flexible work hours. The article was dense, running over 10,000 words (or roughly twice as long as the U.S. Constitution). It seemed ready to drop into obscurity by the sheer weight of its words until a friend of Bundy's spent about $4,000 to mail copies to legislators and journalists. Eventually the story's anti-rail message began resonating with influencers across the region.

Sound Transit felt compelled to respond and in a later issue of the magazine Dave Earling, the Edmonds City Council member and new chair of the Sound Transit Board, penned a rebuttal called "Why Light Rail Works."

Recognizing that it was losing the media and public opinion battle, Sound Transit began mobilizing to fight the war it thought it had already won when its mass transit project was approved by voters in 1996. Using a plan drawn up by Cocker Fennessy, the agency tried desperately to improve its credibility through the final rocky months of 2000. The strategy included creating an internal team of three to five people whose mission was to take the offensive, gather information, write simple talking points, and fire salvos back at critics. The plan called for the team to establish a centralized "rumor-central" where attacks and opposition moves, media records, and emails would be kept for easy retrieval.

In addition, the agency sought to "dominate the news" through special events, news conferences, and releasing positive reports about light rail. An outside group of prominent light rail supporters would be called upon to appear on radio talk shows, draft guest editorials for newspapers, attend editorial boards, meet with opinion leaders, and call the Congressional delegation to express support.

The war room effort looked good on paper, but the team's efforts were drowned out in the rising tide of opposition. Vaska recalled a phone call from Bob White saying: "We need to get the band back together. We're in trouble and we could lose this thing."

In the great Seattle tradition of problem-solving, a committee was formed to study the matter. Former Mayor Charlie Royer chaired the "Project Review Committee," a group of civic leaders assembled to help pilot Sound Transit through the rough waters. Besides Vaska and other leaders, the group recruited Slade Gorton, recently defeated after 12 years in the U.S. Senate. Although he sat on the other side of the aisle from Senator Patty Murray and the Democrats, Gorton was a strong ally of Sound Transit and had rolled up his sleeves for the agency more than once by helping secure federal dollars.

The committee began meeting in late 2000 and continued through 2001 before developing recommendations that included beginning construction as soon as possible on an initial light rail line: "The experience of other cities and counties around the country has been that completion and operation of an initial light rail segment has resulted in strong public support and federal funding for extending the system to other neighborhoods and communities. Promptly starting an initial segment supported by the communities it serves will nurture further support for light rail extensions," the committee wrote in its final report.[2]

In other words, get to work. Now!

• • •

The year 2000 turned out to be a turning point of sorts, although there was scant appreciation of it at the time. Throughout that year some of the most talented engineers the agency would have were hired—Ahmad Fazel, Dick Sage, Joe Gildner, and Henry Cody. And then, on October 9, 2000, Joni Earl walked through the thick wooden doors of Union Station. She didn't know it then, but she would scarcely have a day off until Christmas.

Earl's first assignment was to analyze the agency's organizational structure, so she made the rounds interviewing board members, department heads, and staff. She clearly recalled her first meeting with Greg Nickels, who bluntly informed her he was disappointed in her hire because even though she had a good reputation, she lacked transit experience.

Only a few days into the job her manager instincts began buzzing—and not in a good way. One of her first meetings was with Paul Bay, Link light rail director. As they were going over financial spread sheets, Bay mentioned that the project would be fine if the Sound Transit Board would just get disciplined. He made the point a couple more times before Earl cut in. "What does that look like, the board being disciplined?"

Bay told her that the board kept saying yes to everybody. Earl asked if he'd ever told the board "no, we can't afford it?" Bay replied that "they don't want to hear that."

"Oh my god," Earl thought.

Earl's next move was to track down and study the "infamous green notebook" containing all the Link cost estimates. To Earl, the numbers in that notebook didn't make sense. "They were borrowing from contingencies to do stuff that was scope. I'd never seen that before. I was thinking this problem could be bigger than the tunnel bid problem."

With White's approval, Earl attacked the budget problem with zeal. The day before Thanksgiving she organized a meeting with everyone who had a piece of the light rail cost estimate. Earl remembers sitting at one end of the table in a windowless room off the Great Hall, while at the other end was Tuck Wilson, former light rail director of TriMet in Portland, recently brought in to help the struggling Link system. Most in the room had never met Wilson.

First up was Jeri Cranney, Sound Transit's real estate manager. She and Bay, the light rail director, were going over real estate numbers when Earl recalled Cranney saying: "that's not our number, we never agreed to this number."

Earl asked what she meant. Cranney replied that her department had provided a much higher budget number for the agency to acquire property needed to build the light rail line. In response, Bay told Earl that the number was too high "so we didn't accept it." Earl asked where the light rail department came up with its number and was told they "plugged in the number they needed it to add up to."

Earl glanced at Tuck Wilson and saw his eyes open wide. The table top exercise continued and again and again Earl heard that when a number was too high, it was simply discarded for something lower. Two hours later, she was reeling. After that meeting, Earl and Wilson met for a drink and a serious chat. Earl kept wondering aloud how far over budget the light rail project had drifted. "I just needed to know how big the problem was. Crazy. I'd never run across anything like that in my career."

Soon after, Earl formed a team from Link, including consultants, to help piece together the new bottom-line schedule and dollars needed to build the light rail project. A meeting commenced every evening at 5:30 p.m. in a conference room in the basement of Union Station. The large tomblike area, euphemistically called the "Garden Level," had been the baggage and immigration area for train passengers decades earlier. In the remodel to make Union Station ready for Sound Transit, offices and conference rooms were built in a ring around the basement surrounding an open space filled with cubicles and desks. The place had few windows and was lit by overhead lights. The feeling of being cut off from the outside was palpable. Sheila Dezarn, who was managing the effort to secure Link's federal funding grant, said the atmosphere was intense as the group slowly pieced together the agency, real estate, construction, and management costs. "We went through the project inch by inch mile by mile trying to rebuild all the cost estimates," she said.

Put another way Ron Lewis, who would later become Link's director, said Earl was looking under the hood and challenging everything.

"It wasn't just our tunneling estimates are high or our real estate estimates are low or whatever it was," he said. "She said let's look at every component of this, every phase of the budget, administrative phase, right-of-way phase, design phase, construction phase, construction management, everything. Let's kick the tires and see how realistic we have been. Let's not assume everything is going to go perfectly."[3]

Ann McNeil, who later became director of the agency's government relations team, was impressed by how Earl was able, from the very beginning, to go around the room and get everyone to weigh in. If you've got something to say, she told them, say it. "Her intent wasn't to get people in trouble or lay blame, her intent was to get the information, make sense of it and then fix it," McNeil said.[4]

In November, barely six weeks after Earl arrived at Sound Transit, Link Director Paul Bay resigned.

• • •

Joni Earl's leadership strengths were tempered by real life experience. She was just 24 years old and barely five months on the job when she became Bremerton's assistant city treasurer. She managed a staff of 17, all older women, who had been in the treasurer's office a long time and who she would later describe as "not very happy that this young whippersnapper came in and beat out two of them for the job."

Suddenly it was sink or swim. Straight out of WSU with her degree and a couple of management courses under her belt, Earl did not yet even have her MBA. She had to figure out fast how to earn the respect and trust of a department whose opinion of her ranged from skeptical to antagonistic.

Fortunately, she found Nell Block, a smart experienced professional who must have seen a spark in Earl.

There was a time or two, early on, when Earl recalled walking into the older woman's office nearly in tears: "Nell, nobody likes me, nobody wants to work with me." Earl would sit and listen to Block, who helped her understand that she was being tested, not personally attacked. "Now turn around, go back out there," Block would say. "Don't let them see that you're upset, don't show that you're upset."

Earl eventually realized that many young managers, rather than listening, learning, and even showing some weakness, are too hung up on proving themselves. She would come to understand that you show strength when you also show humility.

So Earl began sitting down one-on-one with her staff at their desks, starting out by saying, "I haven't been here long enough to really know what's going on here, can you show me your job and how you do things?"

She won them over by respecting their tenure, their knowledge, and not acting like at 24 years old she knew everything.

• • •

Earl's initial meetings to uncover light rail's true costs would sometimes last until two or three in the morning. Slowly, like the clouds parting around a mountain peak, the numbers emerged.

Earl remembers the phone conversation she had with Bob White following one of those late-night meetings.

"Bob, you've got a problem," she said. "This is really serious."

"What do you mean?" he asked.

"I think this is close to a billion dollars off."

There was dead silence on the phone.

"Are you kidding me?" he asked eventually.

"No."

On December 14, 2000, after Earl had been on the job only two months, the startling new numbers were released to the Sound Transit Board and the public: it would take three years longer and cost more than a billion dollars more to complete Sound Transit's first light rail line. The news was received first with disbelief, followed soon after with anger.

A strikingly frank letter from Bob White to the board accompanied the bombshell:

> The major question I believe the board should be asking is, why should I believe Sound Transit staff now? You've given the board assurances in the past and they weren't reliable, what's different? Through this process, I, personally, and the agency, in general, have a much better understanding of the honest mistakes and errors in judgment that were made. Most importantly we inadvertently did not serve the board, and therefore the public, as well as they deserve. In the crush to complete the Link light rail project by 2006, staff did not bring everything it should have to the board's attention as early as it should have—including some big issues like how the changing scope was affecting schedule and budget. The staff should have had earlier and more frequent in-depth discussions with the board on cost control, scope creep, cumulative impacts of design choices and changes on project schedule and total cost to complete before the board actions were taken. For that I am truly sorry.[5]

Dave Earling, the new chair of the Sound Transit Board, said the blessing in the destructive whirlwind was that the agency's governing board took the shots and stood united behind the light rail project. That unity, he said, allowed the board leaders to carry the message that "this has been a mess and we're gonna fix it."[6]

Earling recalled how a meeting in a local restaurant with board leaders turned into a "kumbaya" moment.

"We made the judgment that we were going to make this project work, we were going to do what it took to make it work. It was pretty exciting because we all said, you know folks this has to work. We knew the messaging would have to be consistent and strong and we would have to do a hell of a lot of work to get back our credibility."

But as far as credibility for the agency, Earling concluded: "It was flat-out gone."

• • •

The media pounced.

Editorial boards, newspaper reporters, and headline writers tried with gusto to outdo each other with failed train metaphors and death-bed Sound Transit stories. A *Tacoma News Tribune* columnist wrote:

"I could roll out the clichés here, about how the wheels have fallen off Link, about how Sound Transit has become 'The Little Engine That Couldn't. But that would be trite."[7]

The *Seattle Post-Intelligencer* editorial board jumped in: "A pattern of arrogance and less-than-truthfulness, capped by a billion dollar cost jump for Central Link has eroded public confidence to the point that a public re-evaluation of the entire project is needed."[8]

The weekly newspaper *The Stranger* wrote: "It's simply too easy to write headlines lampooning the steadily more ludicrous efforts of Sound Transit to build its central Link light rail system: Train to Nowhere. Tripping the light rail fantastic, The Missing Link, Unsound Transit, Unwise at any speed, pissing away a fortune."[9]

The *Daily Journal of Commerce* wrote: "A chorus of told you so burst out around the region yesterday as news of Sound Transit's vastly increased light rail budget and lengthening project time line circulated among critics of the agency." "What a mess huh?" said Matt Griffin, managing partner of Pine Street Development who has been critical of Sound Transit.[10]

And the neighborhood newspaper *University Herald* simply announced: "Stop the train we want off."[11]

• • •

Agnes Govern, director of Sound Transit's Regional Express bus program, said when the billion dollar number came out "it was just unbelievable, every day there was a headline."

She said it wasn't as if Sound Transit suddenly went from being an agency that was successfully designing and putting out bus service and moving forward on commuter rail to an inept agency that couldn't do anything. "But once something blew in those days everybody drilled down and there were all sorts of stuff. We had the bulls eye on us and it sure felt like it for a long, long time."

Mercifully, the year 2000 was coming to a close. But if the agency and those who worked there thought 2000 was rocky, it was nothing compared to what was coming in 2001.

5

Hope Was Not Our Friend

How could we have gotten it so wrong?
—Rob McKenna

The year 2001 began with a billion dollar question. How could the estimates to build Link light rail be so off?

The auditing firm, Deloitte & Touche LLP, was called in for the official autopsy. Their four main conclusions, even couched in the bureaucratic language of auditors, struck a blunt blow to the agency's image.

1. Sound Transit's preliminary engineering lacked cost estimating guidelines, leading to deficiencies in the estimates. The budget numbers were overly optimistic and counted on the best case scenario; estimates were prematurely reduced by Sound Transit management hoping that reductions would be made up later by savings in other areas. For example, Sound Transit slashed the light rail vehicle cost estimate by $50 million based on the bids receive in a Minneapolis transit project.

2. The budget lacked adequate contingences and those it had were substantially below industry norms. At the same time, the project had many unknowns that were very sensitive to cost increases, such as third party agreements and buying land for the train's right of way.

3. Already low contingencies were reduced even further to create a project reserve.

4. Some estimates relied on insufficient data, most noticeably the lack of testing and geotechnical work needed for the proposed tunnel running from downtown Seattle to the University of Washington.[1]

Those who'd been around Sound Transit a while, or were perceptive newcomers like Joni Earl, had their own views on what happened and why.

Earl summarized the billion dollar problem in three areas: skyrocketing real estate costs, unplanned expansions of the project, and rising administrative costs needed to cover the growth in employees. Sound Transit's finance plan assumed the agency would operate with 100 employees, but by the year 2000 the workforce was 230 and growing. Meeting rooms were converted into offices and, it seemed, new employee badges were issued daily.

Greg Nickels summed up the problem in four words: "The need for speed." The agency was moving so fast to deliver new bus and rail service within the 10-year time frame promised to voters that it took risks, the biggest being the tunnel from downtown to the University of Washington.

It was obvious but still notable that no one had ever before built light rail in the Puget Sound region. The blueprint of how to do it from modern light rail cities like Denver, Dallas, and Los Angeles had limited usefulness when overlayed with Puget Sound's unique geography that required tunnels and bridges.

Brian McCartan, former Sound Transit finance director, said from the beginning the agency was filled with smart, capable people but it was "mission impossible" for a new agency to organize itself from whole cloth and in 10 years successfully launch buses, commuter rail, and light rail trains.

"No matter how much wonderful work was done and how wonderful the work was going…there was going to be a day of reckoning," McCartan said. Surprisingly, one of Sound Transit's greatest strengths, its get-it-done attitude, also contributed to its problems.

"There was a tremendous ethos, commitment from the early crew that we were going to deliver what we promised," McCartan said. That often meant quietly trying to solve problems without raising warning flags up the chain to the board—warning flags that should have been raised.

Looking back, former director Bob White concluded that the Sound Transit staff, the board, and the Puget Sound community were naïve about the magnitude of what the agency was trying to do. People supported light rail in concept, he said, but when it was time for final designs and stations in neighborhoods, everyone suddenly wanted changes. "To those of us, like myself, who had been involved in the planning of this for 10 years prior to the [1996] vote we sort of thought all those studies and all those community meetings and all the lines we drew on the map sort of meant something," he said. "But it went into the communities and it started from scratch."

White recalled that one of the dustups in his relationship with the Sound Transit Board was in 1998, just after Paul Schell was elected mayor of Seattle. "Paul was a big thinker and he saw this big project and said this is something I can influence. Literally, a quote from him at one point was: 'we don't need to be bound by the decisions people made in the past.' I frankly didn't take it well and it was an error on my part not to recognize that it was a sort of natural feeling from somebody who had just been elected mayor of Seattle. He felt he ought to be able to put his stamp on this thing."

Other leaders and communities clamored for changes—some minor, some whimsical, some mind-blowing—that came at the expense of the project's timetable, or Sound Transit's financial health, or even the viability of future ridership. The University of Washington asked that a planned light rail station move nearly a mile from campus to Interstate 5, a proposal that lacked any realistic solution for getting passengers from freeway to campus over car-clogged streets. Tukwila insisted on an expensive new route along I-5, away from its population centers and the transit-dependent neighborhoods that most needed light rail. Tukwila leaders were afraid that running light rail on Tukwila International Boulevard (Highway 99) would ruin their future land use plans for that major arterial. A city of roughly 17,000 residents at the time, Tukwila went so far as to hire a lobbyist to glad hand state and federal decision makers in support of the new route. It worked. Tukwila got its route but it cost taxpayers an extra $50 million, took longer to build, and would forever carry fewer passengers, making it less effective in the long run.

"It was a shame," White said. "But you know there were very few people that demanded things out of evil intent, but the impact of it was a huge increase in cost and schedule."

Former Deputy Director Paul Matsuoka felt that some jurisdictions saw Sound Transit as a gravy train. So, he said, when the UW learned of preliminary plans for a light rail tunnel under a physics lab, the university insisted on special and very costly protections on the theory that the lab might, someday, have instruments sensitive enough to measure that level of train vibration. Others wanted new sidewalks, noise soundproofing, even a new fire truck. King County Metro, the place where Sound Transit was born and shared offices for a time, demanded a king's ransom to turn over its downtown bus tunnel for trains. And so it went, on and on.

"I thought people would be more reasonable," Matsuoka concluded. "I naively thought the people had spoken and said they wanted this. I thought there would be a lot more collaboration."

Ron Lewis, who would later become Link director, joined Sound Transit in 1998 as part of a consulting team specializing in light rail environmental work. He saw an agency trying to launch a huge capital program with tens of millions of dollars in design contracts that, at the same time, was struggling to get its basic administrative policies and procedures in place. "I mean, it was like how do you order paper and pens?"

At one point, problems in the accounting system meant some Sound Transit vendors got stiffed on their payments. Kathryn DeMeritt, one of the agency's first graphic designers, remembered a time when Sound Transit's payments were so tardy a vendor held back desperately needed signage. "It felt like our agency had totally gotten out of control," she said.

By the year 2000 it was obvious to a lot of people that delivering light rail in 10 years was a lost cause. The perception went from hopeful, to unlikely, to remote, to impossible.

Hope, as Joni Earl would conclude, was not our friend.

• • •

The need for speed, real estate right-of-way costs, increased pressure from cities and towns, ballooning administrative costs: there were honest explanations for why it happened, but the region was in no mood to listen.

Rob McKenna, smart and politically savvy, didn't shy away from his outsider role on the Sound Transit Board. The future state attorney general at that time was a member of the King County Council representing East King County, a hotbed of light rail opposition. Others on the Sound Transit Board eyed him suspiciously, feeling that sometimes what was said behind closed doors would find its way into the next day's newspaper.

Former Seattle Mayor Greg Nickels saw McKenna as either Good Rob or Evil Rob. The Good Rob, in Nickels' view, worked with colleagues, regardless of party affiliation, to get things done. "There were a number of places where he and I did that, but the Evil Rob came out on light rail. I'm not saying he wasn't actually philosophically against it, I think at some point he was, so that was an honest position, but the way he went about it was very devious and so it was very difficult. It was difficult to figure out what we can say in this meeting that he's not going to take and twist and so it got a little weird there. It was a little awkward."

From his perspective, McKenna believed that light rail was prohibitively expensive. He advocated for a bus rapid transit system for the Puget Sound region that he believed was not only cheaper to build but would be faster to get up and running.

Regardless of how some of his fellow board members may have felt, McKenna stubbornly stuck with it, asking the staff tough questions. He thought that when it came to light rail, the majority of the board didn't ask enough of those tough questions.

"Agency leadership was manipulating the information about budgets, about reserves, trying to mask that cost estimates were rapidly escalating and that the budget would not work," he would recall. "Agency management was hiding the ball in terms of the financial feasibility of the plan. Management didn't want to deliver the bad news and too many board members weren't apt to fighting it."

McKenna's frustration over the escalating light rail cost boiled over at an early 2001 Finance Committee meeting. At that meeting McKenna, who would later make two serious runs for governor, let it rip:

> I heard one of our board colleagues on the radio or read him in the paper saying, 'oh well, we've had these same concerns, too.' I sure as heck didn't see that board member raising those concerns on January first or last December or November or October or September. We've got to make a commitment that from now going forward we've got to start doing a better job as a board at asking hard questions and not accepting half-baked answers.
>
> Doggone it, we have got to have some answers to the why and if we don't get them I'm afraid we are going to repeat the same errors again. There is no introspection going on here. It's just spin control. That's just not acceptable. Why was our $2.4 billion estimate in November and the fall of 1999 going into 2000 so far off? How could we have got-

ten it so wrong? If I sound frustrated it's because I obviously am. Being a team player means asking the hard questions and being demanding and I doubt that any board member could say with a straight face that we have done an adequate job of that.[2]

• • •

Marketing director Tim Healy was now convinced that Link had morphed from an engineering problem into a dangerous, full-blown political problem.

"There's always an engineering solution to any problem, there are ways to reduce costs, but it's the political side that makes or breaks you," he said. "How do you rebuild that political trust?"

Healy noted that by the beginning of 2001 Sound Transit had few friends. Nobody seemed willing to offer a saving hand as Sound Transit slowly sank. Within the walls of Union Station, that knowledge often felt like the lonely sting of betrayal. "And it wasn't like our partners, King County, or Pierce Transit or Community Transit were clamoring to our defense," Healy said.

6

Dark Winter Malaise

We were fighting not just the political fight, but fighting for
the hearts and minds of the region.
—Ann McNeil

Starting just after lunch and lasting until the sun disappeared behind the Olympic Mountains, the January 11 board meeting was the first of several survival points that defined Sound Transit in 2001.

The Union Station boardroom was packed so full that winter afternoon that portable speakers were hurriedly set up in the nearby Great Hall for the overflow. Inside the room someone unfurled a homemade canvas banner that read "Unsound Transit, not on time, not on budget."[1] Thus the tone was set for the most excruciating marathon the board and staff had ever sat, yawned, seethed, or squirmed through.

At the meeting's end, the board agreed to accept a $500 million federal grant needed to build the light rail project. But, like everything to do with Sound Transit that year, even a simple yes was complicated. The board knew that accepting the federal dollars was like shaking a stick at the swarm of bees swirling around the agency. To refuse or delay, however, would jeopardize the prospect of ever seeing the money, and without it there would be no light rail project. Even with the board's approval the agreement was only half done. The grant still required the signature of the U.S government and—thanks to the latest Link light rail developments—the hand extending the federal money, once steady and sure, was now shaky at best.

Newly elected President George W. Bush would take office January 20 and the government, so supportive of transit projects under President Bill Clinton, now faced tough sledding under the new Republican administration. Strong signals were already coming from influential Republicans in D.C. that the Sound Transit grant money might never reach Seattle. Congressman Hal Rogers of Kentucky, the new chair of the House Appropriations Transportation Subcommittee, would soon ask that the federal grant be frozen until questions about the Seattle project were answered. He also called for a review by the federal Office of Inspector General.

Republican Congresswoman Jennifer Dunn of Bellevue, whose district included parts of Sound Transit, was making her opposition to the federal grant well known in Congress and among power brokers back home. Her opposition would eventually include a pointed last-ditch effort to scuttle the federal grant. In the final months of 2000 and heading into the new year, the schedule for Sound Transit to receive its federal money was slipping and while not quite DOA, the grant was surely giving off an unpleasant odor. Opposition from a sitting congresswoman in the very district the grant was meant to help did not make the smell any more pleasant. "Even to our friends in the Clinton administration it was a hard sell," recalled Peter Peyser, a Washington, D.C., lobbyist hired by Sound Transit for his knowledge of the federal funding program and his contacts throughout the transportation field. "It was very touch-and-go throughout that period. That was very unusual, these things rarely get to that point."[2]

In an attempt to head off opposition, Bob White sent a letter to the Sound Transit Board three days before its January 11 meeting outlining the recent changes at his agency:

> Sound Transit has come to a better understanding of the causes of the current situation and identified better ways to manage the light rail project. More reviews are in place and greater emphasis has been directed on overseeing the project's costs, schedule and scope and on being more open and accountable to the board and the public.

His letter did little to soothe raw nerves. Board members were furious with Sound Transit staff, believing they were misled with rosy details of the light rail project. Even friendly members of the state's Congressional delegation in Washington, D.C., simmered, as did the Federal Transit Administration, the agency in charge of overseeing the federal contract with Sound Transit. At the same time the opposition was energized and on the offensive. Some staffers began covering up their Sound Transit ID badges as they left Union Station to avoid engaging with an angry public. At cocktail parties and across backyard fences, agency employees found themselves on the receiving end of unsolicited advice on solving the light rail problem. On a weekend kayaking trip, all Brian McCartan heard for two days was jokes about Sound Transit.

• • •

A week before the January 11 board meeting, a well-heeled opposition group called "Sane Transit" spent $50,000 for two radio spots lambasting light rail. One ad, read by a professional actress, called Sound Transit a train wreck and urged listeners to flood the agency with phone calls demanding a new vote.[3]

Adding to the pile-on was State Senator Dino Rossi, another Eastside Republican, who introduced a bill in the legislature that would force Sound Transit to ask voters if the agency should be dissolved. The bill went nowhere, but Rossi, who would later twice run unsuccessfully for governor, got his headlines.

And then came the announcement that a group called Ride Free Express had formed to kill light rail and offer free bus rides in its place. The plan seemed to make sense until it was pointed out that the fleet of new free ride buses and vanpools would languish in the same traffic congestion that already existed. And yet the group, including former governors Booth Gardner and John Spellman as well as former King County Metro bus director Chuck Collins, further proposed, with mind-numbing audacity, that Sound Transit divert all its light rail money to Ride Free Express. Gardner's opposition caught Sound Transit off guard given that public transit is generally a bedrock issue among Democrats. Two days later the two former governors again proclaimed their support for Ride Free Express.[4]

Months of such highly visible opposition took hold throughout the region so that alternatives to light rail, like free buses, seemed viable— even though they had already been thoroughly studied and rejected as too costly, lacking serious ridership, or unworkable for Central Puget Sound's unique geography of waterways and steep hills. Local transit planners had long before concluded that light rail trains, using their own tracks free from traffic congestion and flexible enough to run in tunnels, above ground, and at street level, made the most sense.

• • •

Besides light rail, the only other alternative that gained traction in the 1990s was Seattle's elevated monorail, built as a showpiece for Seattle's 1962 World's Fair. The mile-long, rubber-wheeled rail line connecting Westlake Mall with the Seattle Center seemed ripe for expansion following the fair, but nothing came of it. That is until Dick Falkenbury, a Seattle taxi driver who relished tweaking the political establishment and bulldogging his way into the spotlight, drafted an initiative calling for a 40-mile monorail system linking Seattle's four corners to downtown. His initiative on the November 1997 ballot, which did not include a price tag, passed by 53 percent. Suddenly, the monorail seemed a genuine rival to light rail.

"I had started this monorail political movement with very few resources and the hope that it might allow me to build something huge and become famous. If I became rich in the bargain, that would be good too," Falkenbury would later write.[5]

Despite the best efforts of Falkenbury and his band of believers, the monorail saga took several turns over the ensuing years and would appear on the ballot four more times. Finally in 2005 it was disclosed that the latest monorail expansion plan, now shrunk to 10 miles, would cost some $11 billion. This time voters overwhelmingly rejected it and the plan joined all those others on the dusty back room shelf.

• • •

Still, in 2001 many thought the monorail was a workable alternative and it too was part of the atmosphere of opposition that overwhelmed the Sound Transit boardroom the afternoon of January 11. Television news cameras ringed the big meeting room in Sound Transit's Union Station headquarters as one taxpayer after another made their way to the microphone set up facing the board. Public comment had barely begun before the two former governors, Gardner and Spellman, met at the speaker's table.

"I'm not here to chastise or lay blame," Spellman began. "I come here to say let's make sure we're right. Consider if another solution, be it monorail or ride free, is the best solution to our problems."[6]

Others in the audience sought to outdo one another by cobbling together wild metaphors wrapped in the language of disgust. A West Seattle man called Sound Transit a "Mad Hatters tea party" that was built on inverted logic, misleading information, and bureaucratic arrogance. "Light rail is a Trojan Horse that needs to be stopped at the gates," he said. A woman from the Beacon Hill neighborhood said Sound Transit was making Seattle look ridiculous. "I hate it when my city looks ridiculous," she said. Another called for Bob White to resign and then admonished the board to "not get persuaded by money and greed."

After listening to two hours of such comments the board, as expected, voted to accept the federal money. Board member Greg Nickels, who later that year would run for mayor of Seattle against an anti-Sound Transit candidate, said the board had an obligation to voters to do everything possible to keep its promise to build light rail. "It's the responsible thing to do," he said. "No one said it would be easy, but it's the right decision."

Board member Rob McKenna, in his familiar lonely position as dissenter, said big questions needed good answers and he hadn't received the information from staff that made him comfortable voting for the federal money. The state's future Attorney General took the opportunity to land a few more blows to the already wobbly agency.

"One of the things that irritates me is how we get information from staff, how incomplete it often is," he said. "Being asked to sign a binding contract with the federal government, I'm not comfortable with that. It's wrong and inappropriate and I can't vote for it."

McKenna's arguments did nothing to persuade his fellow board members, who voted 14 to 1 in favor of signing the grant. Their decision that day would hang over the agency long after the television and radio crews packed their equipment and the signs were removed from the board room walls.

• • •

The drama of that board meeting in early 2001 made it clear that Bob White's days were numbered. Despite their calm public demeanor no board member, no matter how outwardly thick-skinned, enjoys sitting for hours while angry taxpayers and civic leaders, not to mention

two ex-governors, toss verbal grenades at your agency and, by extension, you. Board members would later point with pride at how they
held together during those tumultuous times.

"The board could have cut and run," Nickels said. "I don't know
how that would have played out, it would have been a disaster, I sup-
pose, it's happened in other cities. But our board, particularly Bob
Drewel, Dave Earling and (King County Executive) Ron Sims, we all
stood and took the slings and arrows."

But privately the board members had had enough. They wanted
change at the top.

Board Chair Dave Earling later noted that although White had
been a "hell of a leader up to that point in the organization," his credibility with the board had slipped. Other board members, including
Nickels, had told the embattled director that his time was up. Of
course, White could scarcely forget the meeting months earlier when
Seattle Mayor Paul Schell leaned over and said: "you know Bob, this
is going to cost you your job."

One Sunday evening around that time Earling remembers
meeting White at a Bellevue restaurant and telling him that he was
"beginning to see the handwriting on the wall." White pulled out his
letter of resignation.

Earling told him: "'Put it back in your pocket because we're going
to find a graceful way out of this,' which relative to the circumstance
I think we did."

• • •

While the board publicly stood steadfast behind the agency, a dark
winter malaise seemed to hang over Union Station and many Sound
Transit employees began updating their resumes.

"The staff was literally fighting for survival and they knew it,"
said Anne Fennessy, the public affairs consultant who found herself at
Union Station more than her own office a block or so away in Seattle's
Pioneer Square District.

Light rail manager Henry Cody remembers a Link staff retreat at
that time in a Lake Washington community center. "Morale at that
point was extremely low," he said. "Tuck [Wilson, acting Link director]

gave some pretty impressive speeches about working on this great public works project and don't lose faith in yourselves. It was helpful, stepping back from the panic of working here day-to-day and reminding people that we're still basically competent and we can still get it done."

But speeches and team building only went so far. Not when you heard nothing but negatives the minute you turned on the news or opened your newspaper.

"There were a lot of folks worried about their jobs, worried about their ability to support their families," said Ron Lewis. "In sports terms it was gut check time because the fate of the agency, the fate of people's jobs and some cases their careers were in the balance and people really had to make some tough choices about whether they were committed to this program and committed to the agency and committed to the mission and committed to each other."

Paul Matsuoka, former deputy director, said Sound Transit was filled with employees who never before had to endure such a constant negative drumbeat. People would come up to Matsuoka, who was a longtime trusted leader, asking if they should be looking for another job. "I was trying to buck them up and said we're trying to change and change is hard, one day we will look back and be proud of what we've done."

Others found a kind of gallows humor. Tim Healy remembers joking that the staff should have had a drinking game where you had to take a sip every time you heard "beleaguered agency," or "troubled Sound Transit."

If so, he didn't have to add, no one at the agency would have been sober.

7

So Close to Dying

Every single day was just wild, just crazy,
the stress level was off the charts.
—Sheila Dezarn

January 19, 2001, the last full day of the Clinton presidency. It was a cold rainy day in the nation's capital as police cordoned off the streets around the White House in preparation for the most elaborate of D.C. traditions: inaugural address, procession, parade, and formal balls.

But while the federal government was undergoing its peaceful transition of power, Sound Transit was much more concerned that day with the unfinished work on its $500 million federal grant. By all accounts the new George W. Bush administration was unlikely to sign the grant agreement—at least not without months and perhaps years of review and delay. As now seemed clear, if the grant had any chance of being signed it would have to be one of the final acts of the Clinton presidency. And time was running out.

"It was a stressful week, and even more stressful day, to say the least," recalled Sen. Patty Murray, who was chair of the Senate Transportation Appropriations Subcommittee.[1] Murray was worried about Sound Transit's budget and schedule woes but believed in the project and knew without the $500 million federal investment there likely would not be a project.

So Murray dispatched her chief of staff, Rick Desimone, along with transportation staffer, Dale Learn, to U.S. Transportation Secretary Rodney Slater's office where they would wait, as conspicuously as possible, for Slater's signature on the grant. Joining them was Pete Modaff, Congressman Norm Dicks' legislative director.

The staffers camped out on a sofa in Slater's office as around them employees boxed up the potted plants, pictures, coffee mugs, and assorted personal memories from the past eight years. As the winter afternoon turned to early evening it was clear that Murray's staffers weren't budging from the couch until the grant was signed—or the clock struck midnight.

Meanwhile, 2,300 miles west in Seattle, Sound Transit leaders huddled in Sheila Dezarn's Union Station office, nervously awaiting word from D.C.

"We were all just sitting in my office dying," said Dezarn, who had been Sound Transit's main architect for shepherding the grant through the tricky federal process. "Bob [White] would come in or Paul [Matsuoka] would come in and Mary Jo Porter [Link deputy director] would come in and Joni would come in and ask, 'What have you heard? What's the latest?'"

Dezarn could only shrug her shoulders. It was past five o'clock, eight o'clock in Washington, D.C., only four hours left in the last day. After decades of trying and more than two years of planning and preparation, to have Seattle's light rail project so close to dying for lack of one signature was becoming more real by the minute.

"As we were ticking down to midnight, it started looking a little dicey that we would actually get this agreement done," said Peter Peyser, Sound Transit's D.C. lobbyist. At that moment, he put the agency's shot at getting the agreement at less than 50 percent.

• • •

It took two full years of equal parts plodding and finesse to bring the Full Funding Grant Agreement (FFGA) this close to signature. Generally such agreements are a behind-the-scenes exercise in paperwork, phone calls, meetings, and deadlines.

In the late 1990s Dezarn, working closely with the Federal Transit Administration (FTA) as well as Sound Transit Board members Bob Drewel and Dave Earling, established a roadmap for obtaining the grant. It was a big ask, half a billion dollars for an agency that had never laid so much as an inch of rail.

Undeterred by the enormity of its undertaking, Sound Transit set a goal of having the grant in hand by January 2001. The process was humming along unnoticed until the summer and fall of 2000 when, with the shocking announcement that the light rail project was three years behind and a billion dollars over budget, it had grown into something very public and controversial.

Peyser said everyone was anxious about the uncertainty of the new Bush administration. "There were going to be new people at DOT, new leadership coming in and at the very least it would have created a very significant pause," he said.

A week before the inauguration Hal Rogers of Kentucky, the incoming chair of the House Transportation Appropriations Subcommittee, sent a letter to U.S. Transportation Secretary Rodney Slater asking him to defer signing the grant so he would have time to understand the agreement and allow its review by the new Bush team.

While externally keeping an increasingly nervous FTA at bay, internally there were discussions at Sound Transit about slowing down or even postponing the federal grant. As Dezarn recalled, "There were moments of serious self-questioning among ourselves about should we still try to get this grant now or do we need to call a big time out and say let's just wait and renegotiate this. There were different voices with different opinions, mine was I think we need to get it, we've got a good project so let's try to get this moving forward." Bob White agreed, saying that it was easier to have a contract and renegotiate it later if you have to rather than starting over from scratch. "It's better to have it than not have it," he concluded.

White, Dezarn, and Paul Matsuoka flew to D.C. in mid-January with the hope of returning with a signed grant agreement. They flew home humbled and empty-handed. "We really went into high gear on trying to figure out how to save the FFGA while the clock was ticking on the Clinton administration," said Peyser, the D.C. lobbyist.

So, with the walls seemingly collapsing in around it, the agency pushed ahead with what was becoming a quixotic quest for $500 million.

• • •

As the hours slipped away on January 19, the reality was there were only three people in the world with the authority to sign the FFGA and they appeared determined to stay as far away from the now toxic Sound Transit as possible. Those three were U.S. Secretary of Transportation Rodney Slater, his deputy secretary Mort Downey, and career FTA official Hiram Walker.

"So here we are, it's January 19, we're not being told anything that gives us real comfort about how this is going to unfold," Peyser said. "I called Mort Downey, it was probably about 7 at night at this point, he was still in the office and Mort and I had known each other for a long time and so I said, 'Mort, how's this going to work?' And he said 'well, you know, we're looking for who's going to sign this document.' I said 'what about the secretary (Rodney Slater)' and he said 'the secretary is at a reception at an embassy right now and we're not even sure he's coming back.' And then I said 'well, Mort, what about you?' He said 'I'm not signing this, this is too hot to handle, this has got to be done at the highest level.'"

When Peyser learned that Transportation Secretary Slater was out of the building and might not return, he became seriously concerned. "At that moment I thought we might be done for. I was living in dread of having to make that phone call to Joni at 9:30 p.m. Pacific time and say the witching hour has passed and we don't have our agreement. I was fully anticipating I was going to have to do that."

But eventually, as the last minutes of the Clinton administration ticked away, Slater returned to the office and in one of his final official acts, signed Sound Transit's FFGA. "It was literally a couple hours to go in the administration so it was really one of the more dramatic moments I've experienced in my 35 year career of doing this kind of work," Peyser said. "It really was amazing."

• • •

In Seattle, where it was now early evening and already dark, Dezarn remained in her office, a sense of dread filling the room. Most employees had gone home convinced the grant would not be signed and feeling that when they returned the next morning the agency would be in serious trouble.

As the minutes ticked away, an email from the FTA finally popped onto Dezarn's computer screen. She opened it. The message she had hoped for had arrived. With a sense of relief more than exhilaration, she quickly sent out emails of her own with two simple words: "It's signed."

Bob White, Paul Matsuoka, and Joni Earl were still in the office when word from Dezarn came. Ron Lewis was with his family at the

Seattle waterfront when he heard. Board member Drewel was sitting on a horse at a charity event at the Evergreen State Fairgrounds in Monroe when Congressman Norm Dicks called to tell him.

Board Chair Dave Earling never forgot the nerve-racking final days of the grant process and how the state's congressional delegation single-mindedly willed it over the top. "Patty (Murray) and Slade (Gorton) were very helpful, we were very fortunate to have had her and Slade. Norm Dicks on the house side was really a giant."

Along with President Clinton's famously controversial 141 pardons he granted that night, the Sound Transit FFGA was one of the last acts his administration ever made. "We were right in there with the pardons," Peyser said. "We had good company."

• • •

Back home, the fallout was swift. A week after the FFGA signing, the federal Office of Inspector General announced an immediate audit of Link light rail focusing on "whether the project is reasonable, what caused the cost overrun and whether any emerging issues might affect its completion."[2]

Such fallout was expected. "People were seriously questioning the judgment of actually doing it and there were people who felt like we had slipped a fast one by having Secretary Slater sign it," Dezarn said. "It takes two years to pull off an FFGA and we got it by the skin of our teeth, but if you walk away from the $500 million there were no guarantees we were going to get it again."

Normally, course-altering news like receiving a half-billion-dollar federal grant would be met at Sound Transit with a celebration, then drinks and back-slapping acknowledgment from peers at a Pioneer Square bar. But there was a feeling among some at the top that the end game was perhaps a little too hardball for congenial Seattle and there was no official celebration.

"It was very odd that way, I think people were ecstatic but it was bittersweet. It was not the celebration it should have been for something so major and so impactful for the region," Dezarn said. "It was almost like getting it, but getting it with shame, which really sucked."

Dezarn left Union Station that night, went home and poured a stiff drink. "I kind of had a moment where I was just exhausted, just really felt wonderful and horrible, it should have been something that was a major career high for me, in some ways it is a career high in that we pulled off a full funding grant agreement under the worst circumstances possible. You talk to people in the industry who were on the outskirts watching it play out, even people back in D.C., they were like 'oh my god, how did you guys do that?'"

The two-year ordeal, particularly how it ended, took a toll on Dezarn. "I had friends come up to my husband and say 'is Sheila going to be ok?' I was a mess. I'm sure I looked like death."

At least for one evening in 2001 Sound Transit felt good. But everyone, including Dezarn, had the sense that the battle for that half billion dollars was far from over.

8

Change at the Top

It is time for the agency to have new leadership that is
unencumbered by past decisions.
—Bob White

When Bob White became Sound Transit executive director in 1995 someone told him jokingly that the "half-life" of such jobs is five years. In other words, half the people in big leadership jobs are out the door in five years or less. "Well," White said as he looked back on his Sound Transit career. "I made it five-and-a-half."

Four days after the federal grant agreement was signed in Washington, D.C., White was gone. Board Chair Dave Earling said change at the top was inevitable. "The credibility of the institution was gone." The end came in a closed-door meeting with the board on January 23, 2001. Long before stepping foot in the boardroom that day, White understood the geometry of his situation.

"I really knew the exit was coming, it was only what was the best timing for the board. One of those was we needed to finish airing the dirty laundry and make sure I was held responsible for all of it," he said. "At that point it was fair. I was, in fact, the one leading it and we were not successful."

Marcia Walker, the longtime board administrator and one of the original 23 Sound Transit employees, was in the room when the board accepted White's resignation. "They talked about who was going to do what and what each board member was going to say," Walker said. "They also talked about making Joni Earl the acting executive director. Somebody asked, 'Does Joni know what's going on?'"[1]

She did not. Earl was upstairs in her office when she received word that the board wanted to see her. Earl remembers heading downstairs and into the boardroom. "They told me that Bob had resigned and wanted to know if I would be acting director." She thought about it for a moment. "I said if I take on the acting job do you have my back because there are a lot of hard decisions in front of you. They said yes, so I said yes. I remember [board member] Cynthia Sullivan asking me 'are you going to apply for the [permanent] job?' I said I have no idea. I don't know what you're looking for, but I'm willing to take it on in an interim basis."

In his resignation letter to Sound Transit Board Chair Earling, White wrote that he was extremely proud of what the agency had accomplished:

> My decision to leave is based on my belief that new leadership can be more effective in restoring public and board confidence in Sound Transit generally, and the Central Link project specifically. It is time for the agency to have new leadership that is unencumbered by past decisions. It is important for Sound Transit to keep moving forward and to fulfill its commitment to the people of this region.[2]

In a separate, more personal email to Sound Transit staff, White wrote that he would miss their day-to-day interactions. "The staff of this agency has been focused and passionate about moving our voter-approved vision ahead. Your dedication and hard work has been an inspiration to me."

The next day, reporters reported and critics crowed.

Under the headline "Transit Chief Resigns" the *Tacoma News Tribune* wrote: "Someone new will have to lead Sound Transit back from the lost confidence and bad publicity that a billion-dollar overrun buys."[3]

Making sure he threw dirt on the grave, Sound Transit opponent Emory Bundy called White: "The symbol of this misguided and star-crossed project. It is past due for him to step aside."[4]

Inside Union Station, before the news was official, even the most unaware staff members knew that their executive director's days were over. The public failings and the drumbeat of bad news were bound to claim careers and the forced resignation of Link Director Paul Bay two months earlier was not enough spilled blood.

Despite what was written in newspaper editorials and shouted on radio talk shows, inside Sound Transit Bob White had always been a much-respected leader. Agnes Govern, director of the ST Express bus program, said White was unique in that he didn't take bad news personally. "His ego was not tied up in it, so you could walk into his office and you could say anything and he would accept it for what it was meant. He was remarkable in that. He's a good man, he really is. And he's just solid in who he is."

Mike Vaska, the attorney who worked with the Seattle Chamber in the early days to bring light rail to Seattle, believed White never got proper credit. "I told people that without Bob White you don't have Sound Transit because without him leading his [original] 23 people, providing the professional focus for the civic work which was also important, we don't get to a second ballot, which by the way was a blowout victory."

White's own assessment was that after the 1996 vote that created Sound Transit the board could have hired somebody with better technical expertise. "I didn't have anywhere near the experience of projects of that magnitude," he said. "What I did bring was organizational skills and I think I did a fairly good job of team building that started a foundation for people to do well."

Immediately following the meeting where she was named acting executive director, Earl hustled upstairs looking for White. She stood in the doorway leading into his third floor corner office with its long polished wood table, large desktop computer, and view of the old Smith Tower in downtown Seattle. His chair was empty, his computer turned off, and his personal belongings gone, as if he knew in advance his time had come.

"It was a sad day," Earl said.

It was also the real beginning of the Joni Earl era at Sound Transit.

9

Are You In, or Out?

She must have wondered at many points, why did I take this job?
—Bob White

The determined clack clack of Joni Earl's high heels announced her arrival long before she turned the corner into what was now *her* top floor office. She was in a hurry. She was always in a hurry trying to save light rail for Seattle.

The clack of those high heels and the purposeful stride projected a confidence that surely was evident for all to see. Inside she was anything but. "I just kept saying we can't fail, we can't fail. You have to figure this out."

This was a new era at Sound Transit and for Joni Earl, it was all Sound Transit all the time—before sunrise, late at night, and most weekends. Her husband, Charlie, who had a high-powered job himself as president of Everett Community College, would bring a change of clothes for those days when she couldn't make it home. In the next few months, there would be five days when she worked 24 hours straight.

Earl was a careful, meticulous manager, an accountant by training, but she knew it was time for action. When your agency is in crisis, wasting time worrying over a thousand and one risks can paralyze a leader. Better to collect the best information you can and then move, move, move.

As Bob Drewel, her longtime colleague said, Earl's exhausting days were necessary, both to salvage Sound Transit and to set the standard for those around her. When the lights in the third-floor northwest corner office burned late into the night, everyone knew the boss was in the building—and she wasn't writing emails to friends.

The first order of business was calling together all Sound Transit directors. Gathered around a table in a Union Station conference room, Earl gave them a blunt assessment of where the agency stood. Then she laid out her core principles—transparency, honesty, open communications, hard work, and complete buy-in of their mission, which was building the region's high-capacity train and bus network. So, are you in or out? "This is what I need to know today if you're going to stay here and help us out of this crisis," she remembered telling them.

The hard-charging Earl knew that some on the leadership team, as well as others throughout the agency, would neither understand nor approve of where she was going. Feelings would be hurt. Managers would be angry. Words would be spoken. Employees would leave. But that was acceptable collateral for what needed to happen. She demanded commitment from her team, 100 percent, or they could find jobs elsewhere "because we are too much in crisis to be dealing with games."

When she took over, Sounder commuter trains and ST Express buses were up and running and although there were operational issues found in any new service, the agency could point to their success. After carrying about a million riders in 1999, ridership jumped to about 4 million in 2000. So Earl left those departments alone and instead lived and breathed light rail, which was the heart of the agency's mission and was on shakiest footing. She knew Sound Transit's survival depended on fixing light rail.

In the first few months of 2001, with Bob White gone and unsure of who she could count on, Earl turned to public affairs consultant Anne Fennessy, who became her interim communications director and confidante.

As former communications director for Gov. Mike Lowry, Fennessy knew the issues and players in the Puget Sound region and had a strong reputation with business and government leaders. She and her business partner, Rick Cocker, had wide experience providing communications strategies for public and private companies ranging from energy and education to transportation. This, however, was an unparalleled challenge.

Fennessy moved from her firm's Pioneer Square offices into Union Station where she would be less than 30 feet from Earl. After a while, that distance seemed to shrink to nothing.

Fennessy calls that time at Sound Transit her "tour of duty." From January to June she and Earl were joined at the hip. They would arrive by five or five thirty every morning, sometimes staying past midnight. And they worked weekends. "We reviewed everything," Fennessy recalled. "We talked probably eight to 10 times a day. It was more than just presentations, it was gut checks, does this sound real, is it believable, who will be mad, who do we need to talk to, can our staff handle this?" There was precious little time, she said, to sit around and "wring our hands."

In the first weeks after taking over, Earl became the face of Sound Transit in the larger Puget Sound community. Now it was Joni Earl who stood in front of the television cameras, met with newspaper editorial boards, and explained Sound Transit to Rotary club luncheons, chambers of commerce, and economic development leaders from Everett to Tacoma. At first blush, Earl did not embrace her new public role. "Fenn [Fennessy] kept saying we need you as the change agent and I said I'm not comfortable with that. She said 'you're the only change in terms of the face of the agency, so you have to own it.'"

Business and community leaders were not necessarily receptive to her or anyone from Sound Transit. Many in the region felt that Sound Transit had betrayed their trust and the natural first reaction was anger no matter who was in charge. "I don't know how many meetings Joni went out to and people wanted to kill her," Fennessy said.

There wasn't much that Earl could draw on in the beginning, but being new at least gave her a clean break from the past. Former director Bob White said Earl figured it out and made it work. "She could say I didn't do this I'm just reporting this, just the facts. It was perfect and she was good."

Making Earl the face of Sound Transit was a smart strategy, said Agnes Govern, director of the ST Express bus program. "It personalized this amorphous Sound Transit. If it had been somebody inept you wouldn't have come up with that strategy and we probably wouldn't have survived, but it worked because of who Joni was."

• • •

Fast and focused attention was also needed to shore up relationships with the Sound Transit Board and the state's congressional delegation. Those regional and national leaders were hearing from constituents and reading front page headlines and, obviously, the front page was not kind to Sound Transit.

In a memo to Earl, Cocker Fennessy warned that Sound Transit's credibility with its Congressional delegation was tenuous: "The DC delegation is still digesting the import of Sound Transit's announcement that Link was $1 billion over budget and would not be finished by 2009." The memo went on to note the "remarkable support" from Senator Patty Murray and Congressman Norm Dicks, adding ominously that "their support will be severely tested over the coming months."

Another memo from Fennessy in early 2001 assessed relations with the Sound Transit Board:

> Strong support from the Sound Transit board is needed, especially over the next six months, for the light rail project to stay on course. Currently, the way information flows to and from the board is unclear and erratic... A well-informed and engaged board will be more likely to support the efforts of Sound Transit staff to move forward with the Link project."[1]

Fennessy recommended the agency adopt a "no surprises" policy and assign a full-time staffer with experience working for elected officials to maintain near-daily contact with every one of the 18 board members. And, in a statement that shows the depth of the damage done, she recommended that the agency "provide all board members with accurate information."

• • •

The new face of Sound Transit was beginning to put her stamp on the place, making changes not just to satisfy internal needs, but that would reverberate all the way to Washington, D.C. As she drew up a workable plan for the future, Earl was brutally honest about past mistakes. She began mending fences with the state's congressional delegation, in particular Senator Patty Murray and Congressman Norm Dicks. Internally, she sought to change Sound Transit's culture.

For a while, the meeting rooms in Union Station had a "naysayer" bucket and anyone called out by their peers for making a negative comment was obliged to toss a quarter in the can. Outspoken staffers would sometimes laughingly throw a couple quarters in the bucket before a meeting even got started. "It was kind of cheesy and it didn't work," recalled Finance Director Brian McCartan. "But it was emblematic of what she was trying to do, which was that the culture needed to change, which was very smart."

Geoff Stuckart, who came to Sound Transit as media spokesman in early 2001on loan from Cocker Fennessy, at first noticed a kind of siege mentality inside the agency. "Your only friend was the person sitting next to you," he recalled.[2]

Internally there was apprehension about Earl, who was an unknown quantity. She had decades of experience running cities and, most impressively, Snohomish County government, but she did not come from the complex world of public transit where the art of maintaining political allies was as important as maintaining budgets. Where were her transit bona fides? Where was her national reputation for rescuing, much less leading, a fledgling light rail system? Once, early on, Earl had to ask a light rail engineer what a TBM was. The engineer was surely shocked given that a TBM—tunnel-boring machine—was the most well-known piece of equipment used to dig light rail tunnels.

Stuckart, who was so hardworking his dinner was often a bag of chips pulled from his bottom desk drawer, became so enamored of Sound Transit he would eventually leave Cocker Fennessy and become a full-time employee. He said it didn't take long for the agency to discover that Earl was more interested in solving problems than cleaning house. "You identified a problem, owned up to it and fixed it," he said. "That was really cool and I think that came across pretty quickly."

At one point in 2001 with employees working long hours in difficult circumstances, it was announced there would be no wage merit increases for the year. Board Chair Dave Earling remembers the all-agency staff meeting where he announced it. "My closing line was 'hold your heads high, keep doing what you're doing because you are good people doing good work.' That was an important time for me because I could see that staff wanted to believe it themselves and believe in themselves but they also knew there would be a hell of a load to pull."

• • •

Before long Earl became as adept addressing internal staff issues as she was describing light rail details to cynical reporters. But when she looked back at those early days, she's not sure how she managed to survive. "It was coming from every angle and I was putting a lot of pressure on myself to figure it out. I was scared. I had a board that wanted us to be successful and were supporting me and backing me and they were all important elected officials and I didn't want to fail them. I think I was running on adrenaline. I'd never dealt with anything this big and I think all of that was what got me through."

10

Sharks Circling

It was blood in the water and the sharks were circling.
—Mike Vaska

Before he left Sound Transit in 2018, the most incongruous item in Finance Director Brian McCartan's corner office was a weird wooden devil. The squat homemade demon with painted red horns and dollar-sign eyes had been left behind years earlier after a contentious meeting in Seattle's Rainier Valley.

McCartan, who "has a good eye for kitsch," carried the devil back to his office where its malevolent stare was a constant reminder of Sound Transit circa 2001. That someone would spend hours cutting, nailing, painting, and then dragging the ugly wooden devil to a Sound Transit community meeting symbolized the dedication of those opposed to light rail. Underestimating their anger was a mistake.

By the time Sound Transit announced that its light rail project was a billion over budget and three years late, critics had the region's full attention. And then it was open season. "There was no appreciation of how vehement the opponents would be," McCartan said. But when the trouble started, "they knew we were on the ropes and they had a chance to strangle it in the crib."

In 2001, at least eight entities were organized to fight Sound Transit, including Sane Transit, Ride Free Express, Citizens for Mobility, the Transportation Legal Defense Fund, Coalition for Effective Transportation Alternatives, Friends of the Monorail, Public Interest Transportation Forum, and Save Our Valley.

They stormed the castle through every unguarded gate. They poured over Sound Transit documents, met with reporters, attended meetings, made phone calls, sent emails, and called radio talk shows. They were persuasive, logical, serious, overbearing, and often annoyingly persistent. In a flyer, one of the groups, the Transportation Legal Defense Fund, heated the rhetoric to boiling:

If the words light rail conjure up an image of a harmless child's train set in your mind, then you would surely be shocked at the reality of these multi-ton, steel-wheeled behemoths as they vibrate, thunder and screech at up to 50 miles per hour, roaring directly under our homes.[1]

The opposition attracted the occasional crazies and kooks, but also a good share of community and government leaders, neighborhood activists, and two former governors. John Niles, a transportation researcher and consultant, was also co-chair of Seattle's Coalition for Effective Transportation Alternatives, whose mission was and remains to promote "cost-effective telematics-based solutions like bus rapid transit and intelligence transportation systems rather than multi-billion dollar symbolism like Sound Transit's Central Link subway, the most expensive light rail per-mile in world history."[2]

Niles recalled that in the early days the opposition to Sound Transit was more fragmented than cohesive.[3] But despite differences in style and temperament, they were united in purpose. The opponents included Tim Eyman, who had transitioned from selling watches to WSU fraternities and sororities to selling voters on his statewide anti-tax initiatives. His carnival barker showmanship would compel Eyman to appear at various press events dressed as a gorilla, Darth Vader, or Buzz Lightyear. He found Sound Transit an easy foil and hung his initiatives around the agency time and again, but for all the bluster, he would fail to cut off tax dollars or prevent the agency from extending light rail.

Geoff Stuckart, who was handling media relations for Sound Transit, remembers when Eyman made a public records request for copies of emails from every employee in the agency. It took days of staff time to pull the mammoth request together. Finally, the records were assembled and carted into a conference room off the Main Hall at Union Station where the serious work of digging through each email would surely take Eyman weeks.

"There were boxes of documents down there for him," Stuckart said. "I mean stacks and stacks and stacks and stacks of paper, more than anyone could look for and he came in one afternoon flipped through it for about 15 minutes and was done."

Eyman wasn't alone in requesting mountains of public records. Washington state law requires that public agencies make their records and documents, including emails, available for public inspection. Few exemptions are granted. In 2001 alone nearly 2,000 pages of requests were processed at Sound Transit.

Others fighting Sound Transit included Sane Transit, a band of well-placed critics organized to oppose light rail when it was first put to voters in 1995 and 1996.[4] Besides Rob McKenna and Emory Bundy, the group included King County Councilmember Maggie Fimia and Seattle City Councilmember Nick Licata.

Ride Free Express, which advocated siphoning light rail money into fare-free buses, enjoyed instant credibility because its founders included former governors Booth Gardner and John Spellman and former Metro bus director Chuck Collins.

McKenna, who later fought light rail from his seat on the Sound Transit Board, said the opposition was an ad hoc group of citizens who cared about transit and wanted to make sure public investments would maximize ridership. Foes like Emory Bundy, he said, were formidable because they were analytically smart, could do the math, read financial reports, and understood light rail engineering.

The language of opposition soon spread from board rooms and newspapers into neighborhoods. Rebecca Roush, who handled non-English communications for Sound Transit, felt the anger and fear in Seattle's Rainier Valley, home to at least 11 languages. The common narrative in the valley was that light rail, which would run at street level down Martin Luther King Jr. Boulevard, was out to destroy neighborhoods and livelihoods. Many Rainier Valley immigrants were from Southeast Asian countries where, Roush pointed out, government was not just dysfunctional but oftentimes murderous. "We were viewed as government, therefore not to be trusted."[5]

While some opponents were harmless gadflies enjoying the sport of tweaking big government, the laser-like dedication of others bordered on fanatic. Emory Bundy spent 12 hours a day, sometimes more, trying to kill light rail.[6] He would file request after request for public records that he would then scrutinize like an overzealous auditor, convinced that Sound Transit was deliberately exaggerating ridership projections, underestimating costs, and making misleading promises.

Soon enough a stream of detailed emails would fly out of Bundy's home computer to a growing network of supporters, community leaders, politicians, and reporters. Sometimes the reporters followed up with stories that would more often than not publicly embarrass the agency. If so, mission accomplished.

Fit and energetic at 64 years old, Bundy was a soccer player and avid bicycle commuter whose career included directing public affairs for Seattle television station King Broadcasting and later the Bullitt Foundation, an environmental action organization headquartered in Seattle. A *Seattle Times* profile relayed how he quit the Bullitt Foundation in 2000 to concentrate his attention on fighting light rail. In August of 2000, his crusade took him to Washington, D.C., where he would lobby Congress and the U.S. Department of Transportation to stop federal money for Sound Transit.

Bundy's animus towards light rail was traceable back to the early 1980s when he directed a King-TV staff that covered the Washington Public Power Supply System's disastrous adventure to build five nuclear power plants in the state. It was a massive failure leading to a $2.2 billion municipal-bond default, the largest in the nation. Even its acronym was unfortunate, given that everyone pronounced WPPSS "whoops." Bundy saw an equivalent debacle in light rail and took to calling it "WPPSS on wheels."

Joni Earl, still new on the job at Sound Transit, remembers when Bundy and former Gov. Booth Gardner visited her office in the winter of 2001 trying to convince her that light rail would never justify the cost. "I listened and took notes, didn't say much," Earl recalled. "They were just full of themselves. They felt for sure this was going to kill the light rail project and Sound Transit as an agency."

Three days after that meeting at Union Station, Bundy sent a follow-up email of around 1,500 words that reiterated, point by excruciating point, his opposition to light rail. As if to underscore his obsession, the tome arrived at Earl's office computer at 4:26 a.m. on a Saturday morning. And then, just 10 minutes later, another email from Bundy arrived, this one a relatively succinct 488 words. It began: "It pains me to be oft-described as a light-rail critic, because it is so negative. My long and energetic participation in this field has been affirmative."[7]

Former director Bob White acknowledged that Bundy accomplished a lot of good throughout his career. But, he would add, "I don't know why he got this bee in his bonnet about light rail."

Seattle attorney Mike Vaska, who for many years had advocated for Sound Transit from his perch with the influential Seattle Chamber, had mutual soccer friends with Bundy and noticed that Bundy had them convinced that Sound Transit was evil. "I would see them on the soccer pitch and they would talk to me about it and I would say you know you can agree with this stuff or you can disagree with this stuff but it's not the devil incarnate. I'm telling you these guys [at Sound Transit] are doing what they think is the right thing to do, they're not going to get it right every time but this is not an evil empire."

Vaska talked to Bundy about respectful opposition because he believed Bundy had legitimate views and could make the project stronger. "Part of my message to Sound Transit…was that the opposition was not evil, some of them maybe, but most just have a different view and don't totally tune them out because they disagree with some aspect of the project. It's the old 'get everyone you can in the tent and then exclude only the ones who are going to kick down the tent.'"

Across Lake Washington in Bellevue, Kemper Freeman was stomping all over the tent. Freeman wasn't officially connected to any opposition group—he didn't have to be, he was a force unto himself. The wealthy owner of the Bellevue Square shopping mall and other valuable Bellevue real estate holdings was never shy about trashing light rail. For him, after all, it was the automobile, not transit trains, that defined the American dream.

Freeman, a former state Legislator who could be by turn generous, charming, blunt, frustrating, and stubborn, said he once spent more than 30 percent of his time on the issue of light rail.[8] He was a keynote speaker at a national American Dream Coalition conference. The anti-light rail organization that defines its mission as "Defending freedom, mobility and affordable homeownership," believes "the automotive revolution played a critical role in reducing poverty, improving health care, and otherwise greatly improving the lives and lifestyles of Americas [sic]."[9] Not much room for transit in that dream.

When he was director of Sound Transit, Bob White recalled a series of breakfast meetings he had with Freeman and credited him for "well-documented and cogent arguments." But he said all those arguments fell apart when you examined the astronomical cost of buying property and getting neighborhood support to actually expand freeways. "Kemper thought you could build freeways to carry more people and technically you could, but politically and community-wise you're not going to do it."

The tactics and talking points for killing light rail in Central Puget Sound were part of a national toolkit provided by groups like the American Dream Coalition. But Ric Ilgenfritz, Sound Transit's former planning and communications director who was schooled in D.C. politics from his days working for Senator Murray on Capitol Hill, said the edge in the Puget Sound region might have been a little sharper because Kemper Freeman was so committed and so willing to use his deep pockets to bankroll the opposition.

Bob Watt, who at the time was CEO of the Seattle Chamber, knew Freeman from earlier days when Seattle was more like a small town. Freeman, he observed, was convinced that roads and buses, not light rail, would improve the transportation network. "After many hours of conversation with Kemper I could tell that logic was not necessarily going to prevail in the conversation," Watt said. "When Kemper gets the bit in his teeth about something he was not going to back down. He sincerely believed it and he had plenty of money to finance the 'no' campaign and he took a lot of his buddies with him. They were spending money like crazy to keep the drumbeat going. When people believe it in their heart and they have resources and they are determined, they'll not likely change their mind."

Ilgenfritz said that once light rail stalled in late 2000, the opponents' narrative became the counter-narrative to Sound Transit. And, he added, the opponents got the benefit of the doubt. "Whatever they said media representatives would bring to us and say Emory Bundy said this, what do you say to that? John Niles would say you guys are terrible for the following six reasons, do you dispute that?"[10] The agency's strategy with the media was to counter with a question of its own: "So should we just do nothing, should we fold the tent and not do mass transit here?" That question, Ilgenfritz said, brought the argument back to the need for transit, which was a winning argument in the traffic-clogged Puget Sound.

Greg Nickels, former Seattle Mayor and original Sound Transit Board member, believed the issue boiled down to light rail being a transformational project. He said:

> When you and I are old and gray we're going to see incredible change in the neighborhoods that are served by the light rail....it's a transformational project and people fear change. Until they can see it and touch it, smell it and taste it you are going to have people who are reacting and I think that was a big part of it. Then, the second piece was they were validated by our missteps. But over time they became less and less credible because they made statements and assertions that simply didn't pan out as we got our act back together as Joni, as leader of the agency, rebuilt that credibility.

11

Persona Non Grata

Just do your job.
—Governor Booth Gardner

Before it got better, it got personal. When former Governor Booth Gardner took on the Sound Transit Board in an April 2001 *Seattle Times* opinion piece he punched hard:

> So, where are the elected officials serving on the Sound Transit board and supposedly protecting our interests? The board chair, Dave Earling, is an active, strong and articulate defender of light rail. But the question persists, why wasn't he aware of the rot inside the organization—and if he was, why did he remain silent. And Finance Chair Greg Nickels must have been briefed as well. If so, why didn't he bring the problems, particularly the glaring cost overruns, to light?...Do we ask the board to resign? No. It would suffice if they would just do their job.[1]

Rot inside the agency? Just do your job? It was as if the opponents had opened a vein and poured all their venom into Booth Gardner's pen. His public lashing was unheard of in local politics—particularly from a Democrat commenting on a public transit project that was overwhelmingly favored by his party.

Earling, a Republican, fired off a response in the *Everett Herald* under the headline "Light Rail Critics Complain a Lot, But Offer Few Alternatives." He wrote, "Honest disagreement on major public issues is a tradition in the Northwest. Personal attacks are not."[2]

The 18-member Sound Transit Board, made up of 17 elected officials from cities and counties along with the Washington State Secretary of Transportation, represent three counties and 53 cities in a district that stretches 1,080 square miles in the most urban area of the state. Their job is to set high-level policy for the agency, but in 2001 it also meant taking heat from old friends and influential elite who were extremely unhappy about what was coming out of Union Station in Seattle.

In the early days the board, like the rest of the agency, believed in great possibilities, said Marcia Walker, who led an internal Sound Transit team that focused on board management. "Of course we can do this, we are Central Puget Sound, this is what we do. We were innocent. The board was innocent."

By 2001 that innocence was replaced by hard-boiled realism. When a Seattle legislator used Sound Transit as an example of transportation funding during a session in the state capitol in Olympia that year, the roomful of lawmakers burst into laughter. "Such is the fame of Sound Transit's failures," a *P-I* statehouse reporter quipped.[3]

Earlier, a group of 15 Republican state legislators published a letter in the *Seattle Times* bemoaning the "loss of trust in Sound Transit."[4] The legislators called for, among other things, a public re-vote on whether or not Sound Transit should even exist. The letter was viewed as political grandstanding by many in Sound Transit who pointed out that although the agency was created by the legislature, the state contributed zero dollars to its operation. Those legislators, in other words, had no skin in the game.

Ric Ilgenfritz remembered the feeling of being on an island. "We were alone, nobody wanted to help us," he said. "We were persona non grata down there [in the legislature], we were literally a punching bag. Every legislator in Olympia who supported our legislation and got us to the ballot paid a political price for being wrong about the RTA [Sound Transit's legal name] and that made them very very mad. So Democrats were super pissed off because they felt we pulled the rug out from under them and Republicans were empowered, emboldened."

• • •

Leading the Sound Transit Board's defense was Dave Earling, an Edmonds city councilmember who also happened to be a skilled leader and effective spokesman. While Joni Earl was the face of the agency staff, Earling was the face of the board. "In my own analysis, I was probably a good person to have as board chair then because the pressures would have been different if Drewel [Snohomish County Executive] or Sims [King County Executive] would have been chair, it would have been a more trying political atmosphere because they had potential for higher office. So maybe it was better to have someone like me, someone on the front lines all the time."

Rick Cocker, co-founder of the public affairs firm Cocker Fennessy, said although Earling didn't have the high visible political standing as some on the board, he devoted a tremendous amount of time and dedication to Sound Transit. Earling's strategy was to build back credibility for the agency by appearing at public meetings, speaking to influential groups, appearing on radio talk shows, and visiting newspaper editorial boards around the region where his message was about how the agency was changing. Mostly the exchanges were polite. Still, Earling never forgot the time a KIRO radio host deliberately made him look bad for several days by re-airing out of context sound bites from their interview.

But for all the negative the board pushed back positive. And, most importantly, they worked together, which meant their own political futures were tied to an agency filled with uncertainty.

"The board really got behind the whole thing," Earling said. "They stuck together and allowed for me and some of the other board members to really carry the message and say this has been a mess and we're going to fix it. It was a great experience to go through, frankly, one that I wouldn't want to re-live, but it gave me a good insight into the kinds of leadership you need to have if you're going to pull together a project that was upside down. None of the board members ran from it, it was a great exercise in a painful way to learn about leadership."

Urban rail transportation is nothing new to Seattle. This photo, taken in 1907, shows a Madison Street Cable Railway car running on Madison at Third Avenue. The Madison Street Cable Railway ran from 1890 to 1940. *MOHAI, Seattle Historical Society Collection, SHS915*

The original Regional Transit Authority (RTA) employees pose for a picture. The RTA became Sound Transit following a successful vote in 1996. *Photo courtesy of Sound Transit*

Greg Nickels, former Seattle Mayor and Sound Transit Board chair, was an early and ardent supporter of light rail in Seattle and Central Puget Sound. He is seen here speaking at a celebration for the opening of light rail in July 2009. *Photo courtesy of Sound Transit*

The Great Hall in Union Station is the open public space in Sound Transit headquarters. Sound Transit bought the long abandoned train depot, built in 1911, for $1 and then spent around $21 million on renovations. *Photo courtesy of Sound Transit*

Joni Earl, Sound Transit CEO, celebrates in her office in 2003 after signing the long-awaited $500 million federal grant assuring construction of the first light rail line in Seattle. *Photo courtesy of Sound Transit*

U.S. Sen. Patty Murray speaks at the Link light rail groundbreaking in November 2003. Murray is a strong supporter of Sound Transit and helped guide it through the federal land mines in Washington, D.C. *Photo courtesy of Sound Transit*

A construction worker watches as the giant tunnel boring machine cutter head breaks through the Beacon Hill light rail tunnel in 2008. *Photo courtesy of Peter de Lory©*

Construction crews at work inside the mile-long Beacon Hill light rail tunnel. *Photo courtesy of Sound Transit*

Working on the tracks heading into the Beacon Hill
Tunnel. *Photo courtesy of Peter de Lory©*

Ric Ilgenfritz, Sound Transit Planning Director, at a light
rail construction groundbreaking event. *Photo courtesy of
Sound Transit*

An elevated span of light rail line goes up and over busy highway lanes as construction continues to Sea-Tac Airport. *Photo courtesy of Peter de Lory©*

A new stub tunnel was built for light rail trains running underneath downtown Seattle. *Photo courtesy of Peter de Lory©*

Joni Earl, Sound Transit CEO, and Ahmad Fazel, Link light rail director, share a happy moment during opening day of light rail service in July 2009. *Photo courtesy of Sound Transit*

Sound Transit Boardmembers Claudia Thomas and Bob Drewel take their first ride on Link light rail's opening weekend. *Photo courtesy of Sound Transit*

Ron Lewis, who would become Link light rail director, speaks during a Sound Transit event at a light rail construction site. *Photo courtesy of Sound Transit*

Former Sound Transit Board Chair Dave Earling, who was an important part of the early history of the agency, flashes a smile onboard a light rail train on the day service began. *Photo courtesy of Sound Transit*

Sound Transit staff members gather in Union Station's Great Hall to celebrate the launch of light rail service in 2009. *Photo courtesy of Sound Transit*

12

Time to Pull the Plug

When big projects fail, this is how they die.
—*Seattle Times*

At exactly 10:54 a.m. on February 28, 2001, Union Station started shaking.

When the small portable television on the office shelf above him began careening wildly, agency spokesman Geoff Stuckart ducked under his desk and held on. At work stations all around him other Sound Transit employees also scrambled for cover.

Kathryn DeMeritt, a Sound Transit graphic designer, looked up from under her shaking desk to see a computer wobbling across a nearby counter. She reached up, pulled down her desk phone and began frantically dialing schools for updates on her young son and daughter.

The shaking lasted 40 seconds, every agonizing tick a lifetime for those feeling the earth buckle beneath them. Would the station's hundred-year-old brick walls hold? Would the ceiling come tumbling down upon them?

David Beal was meeting with Joni Earl in a third-floor conference room when the Nisqually Earthquake struck. It was the first sizeable earthquake in the Puget Sound region since 1965. They dove under the table and rode it out. In the nearby Opus East office building where Link light rail employees and consultants had moved to ease crowding in Union Station, filing cabinets began tumbling over. Work mates rushed outside and gathered together on sidewalks, gaping wide-eyed at the drama playing out around them.

The earthquake, measuring 6.8 on the Richter scale, was centered near the Nisqually Delta northwest of Olympia but felt as far away as Vancouver, British Columbia. The hardest hit buildings included Seattle's Pioneer Square, home to Sound Transit, the International District, Safeco Field, and the Seahawks' new football stadium, then under construction. Immediately following the quake two workers suspended high atop the stadium's steel infrastructure could be seen swinging precariously on a scaffold. Brick fascia and cornices toppled from Pioneer Square buildings, crushing parked automobiles underneath. All told more than 200 injuries were reported across the region. A woman in Burien suffered a heart attack during the quake and, because of jammed phone lines, her husband could not contact emergency services in time to save her.

The brick walls held and Sound Transit's buildings sustained minor damage. Still, Union Station's historic Great Hall would remain closed for months as specialists carefully repaired cracks in the ornate ceiling and walls.

Not long after the quake Link engineers were called upon to assure a skittish region that light rail tunnels are safe, even safer than above ground in an earthquake with its falling bricks, glass, trees, and power lines.

As the engineers would point out, the Bay Area Rapid Transit tube running under San Francisco Bay to Oakland was one of the few transportation systems operating right after the devastating Bay Area earthquake of 1989. In San Francisco, BART trains were running and stations were open. Just like they would be in Seattle, Sound Transit engineers said. Trust us. But the earthquake gave skeptics yet another reason to question the light rail plan.

The Nisqually Earthquake was only one in a series of gut punches to the region that winter. Central Puget Sound was growing up and with it the uncertainty of change.

In March Phil Condit, the Boeing Company CEO who had so enthusiastically endorsed Sound Transit five years earlier, announced that company headquarters were moving from Seattle to Chicago, leaving behind the only home it had known since 1916. The stunning news was felt as far away as the East Coast where the *New York Times* sent a reporter to see what was going on in the faraway reaches of the Pacific Northwest. If the theme of the article was unrest, the reporter found plenty of supporting examples:

> Microsoft is fighting an antitrust battle. The go-go dot-com economy is sagging, with the stock of Amazon.com, RealNetworks and other Seattle Internet companies in steep decline. There has been an earth-

quake and a drought. And now Boeing, the biggest employer in the region, plans to move its headquarters somewhere else.[1]

The article was peppered with quotes about how Seattle had grown into a big city along with inflated housing costs and coarsening culture. For old timers, the place seemed to be turning its back on legendary "Seattle nice."

• • •

Earthquake restoration crews were still hard at work in the Great Hall in April when the federal Office of Inspector General released its 15-page interim report on Link light rail. Three months earlier, Congressman Hal Rogers of Kentucky, the new chair of the House appropriations subcommittee that oversees the distribution of federal transportation dollars, had asked the nonpartisan Inspector General to review Sound Transit's $500 million federal grant. The IG office, which is the auditing arm of the U.S. Department of Transportation, went to work straight-off, looking not just at Link but the oversight role of the Federal Transit Administration.

The earthquake had done little to shake the IG's zeal for the job. Details of the report were leaked to the news media at the same time it arrived at Sound Transit. Before the agency had time to digest the findings, reporters were already burning up the phone lines. The report was a scorcher.

Inspector General Kenneth Mead wrote that a number of outstanding or unresolved issues warranted prompt action by FTA and Sound Transit. Several of those issues, he wrote, should have been settled prior to executing the grant agreement. "We are recommending that funds and funding decisions for the Project be held in abeyance until the Secretary of Transportation determines the FTA has resolved these issues and Congress has had time to review the grant agreement."[2]

Held in abeyance, on ice, on hold…no matter how it was said, the effect was transformational for Sound Transit. The very next day Norman Mineta, the recently appointed U.S. Transportation Secretary and essentially the top transportation official in the nation, announced that all federal funds for Link were on hold. The announcement read: "In the interest of good stewardship, we cannot commit taxpayers' money until it is determined that the FTA and Sound Transit have satisfactorily addressed the issues raised in the Inspector General's report."[3]

The IG's concerns fell into three areas.

1. The FTA did not perform satisfactory due diligence in the grant's review process.

2. The FTA's December 2000 review of the Link project, including its examination of the higher cost estimate, was not thorough enough to allow for the last-minute approval of the federal grant in January 2001.

3. Changes to Link's scope, cost, and schedule estimates resulted in opposition to and confusion about the project.

In its reporting the next morning, the increasingly aggressive *Seattle P-I* claimed the action was "striking a potentially fatal blow to the faltering project." The newspaper went on to quote Congressman Hal Rogers as saying: "This report finds that both the Federal Transit Administration and Sound Transit failed in providing due diligence to this project—a basic responsibility expected by those who pay federal, state and local taxes. It's clear that the full funding grant agreement itself was indeed premature with numerous, basic questions about the project left unanswered."[4]

In his own press release that day, Congressman Rogers would not mince words:

> During the final hours of the Clinton Administration, I strenuously objected to Secretary Slater's headlong rush to commit the federal government to a full funding grant agreement for Sound Transit. At that time, there was growing evidence that the project just wasn't ready for such a significant step. Today, DOT Inspector General Ken Mead, in his interim report on Sound Transit, has underscored those concerns.[5]

To local light rail opponents, Rogers became like a faraway folk hero in the crusade to cudgel Sound Transit. Around that time a man showed up at a Sound Transit Board meeting, pulled out a half-empty bottle of Kentucky bourbon, raised it towards Sound Transit's leadership and gave thanks to Hal Rogers. He left soon after, carrying away his bottle of precious bourbon.

No matter how it was spun, the Inspector General's report was a trip to the woodshed for Sound Transit. The only ray of sunshine on the way to that woodshed, and it would turn out to be significant, was that instead of completely cutting off Link light rail and making the agency start over and re-apply for its federal grant, Mineta agreed to hold Sound Transit's federal dollars in place until it proved its worthiness. That was the opening Sound Transit needed and would prove the salvation of the agency.

Peter Peyser, Sound Transit's lobbyist in D.C., believed it was the agency's incredibly good fortune that President Bush appointed Mineta, the lone Democrat in the new President's cabinet. Mineta was a former Congressman from California and chair of the Transportation Committee. Particularly fortuitous for Sound Transit was that Mineta was a big proponent of public transportation, was friends with many in the Washington State congressional delegation and, Peyser said, knew the major players in the region. Peyser was certain that almost any other U.S. Transportation Secretary would have slammed the door shut on Sound Transit. "He (Mineta) essentially comes in and says I'm going to hold this $500 million for you. We're going to park it and we're not going to give it to anybody else and it's there for you if you can get this thing back on track."

• • •

For transit agencies across the country, the federal grant process is like lining up for a bank teller. When you first apply for federal dollars you're at the end of the line. Eventually, as other projects across the country receive their dollars, you move up. What Mineta told Sound Transit was, in effect, we'll hold your place in line, but you've got to prove that you've made the changes necessary to allow you to get your cash.

For Earl, proving it meant a flight to Washington, D.C., every couple of months to win over a suspicious, closed-fisted federal government.

After totaling up her trips to D.C., she recalled a local headline titled "Mrs. Earl Goes to Washington." Earl wasn't looking for frequent flier miles. She was going back to meet the state's congressional delegation and federal transportation leaders trying to smooth over the rough spots. "I needed the Inspector General to know that I was all over the audit and I needed them to know that we were taking it seriously," she said. "I needed to shore up the congressional delegation, let them know we were taking all these steps." The end game was making sure Sound Transit secured its $500 million federal grant.

"Unless we got that grant," Earl had concluded, "we were dead."

• • •

One Friday afternoon, after she had tried unsuccessfully to land a meeting with Secretary Mineta, Earl was at Reagan Airport near downtown Washington, D.C., awaiting a flight home. All at once she heard a familiar voice booming behind her: "Joni Earl! Joni Earl!"

She turned. Congressman Norm Dicks was gesturing at her. "Joni," he told her when she'd caught up to him. "You've got a meeting with Norm Mineta in 45 minutes."

Earl told the Sound Transit staff traveling with her to continue on back to Seattle. "You guys fly home, I'm going to start figuring this out."

Dicks had interceded, scheduled the meeting with his former congressional colleague and even went so far as to track Earl down at the airport. Earl, thankful for Dicks' help once again, hurriedly retrieved her luggage and taxied back to the city, flipping through the gears in her head for what to say and how to say it.

She needn't have worried about how she'd come across. After less than six months at Sound Transit, Earl already exuded the confidence of the over-prepared. She asked questions and absorbed the answers, never needing to hear information twice. Her accountant's ability to digest numbers, along with highly developed social and political skills, helped more than once in dealing with top-of-the-org-chart temperaments.

She walked into Mineta's office that day and exchanged greetings. He had a tablet in front of him and a piece of paper under the tablet. She never forgot his words.

"I will not have fraud or waste on my watch," he told her.

"Neither will I sir," she replied.

The two shook hands and a friendship was born.

Mineta began giving Earl advice on how to maneuver around the hidden perils of the Inspector General investigation. He gave her the names and numbers of top people at agencies who had been through similar investigations and she was smart enough to follow his advice.

On another trip to D.C. that spring Earl met Inspector General Kenneth Mead for the first time. She remembers, "I had to talk a mile a minute because he wasn't listening to me and whenever I got an opening I just went blah, blah, blah, blah, blah and finally he sat back and let me talk about the agency and what had happened. I kind of won him over in that meeting."

Mead explained how an IG audit works and told her to expect auditors to be around full time in Sound Transit offices for a while, which they were, and probably longer than anyone expected. The interim report led to another, much more intense Inspector General examination and soon federal auditors took up shop in Union Station's basement level. The IG wouldn't finish up its Sound Transit audits until 2003.

"They descended on us and lived with us for quite a while," recalled Brian McCartan, then Sound Transit's deputy finance director. McCartan and Hugh Simpson, the agency's finance director, spent countless hours filling data requests and fending off challenges. After a while, it seemed clear to McCartan that the auditor's marching orders from D.C. weren't so much to help the agency as to hunt out fraud and abuse of public funds.

"That was painful," McCartan said. "It had the aura around it of criminal intent. These guys were looking for shady accounting or something. They never did find anything because there wasn't anything, but that was the worst part for me, feeling like you were under federal investigation. That was not fun."

• • •

During those hectic first months of 2001, Earl candidly told the *Seattle Post-Intelligencer* that the grueling work schedule and negative publicity was causing morale problems at the agency. "We're burning out staff right now," she said.[6]

Key departures included interim light rail director Tuck Wilson, deputy director Mary Jo Porter, and the agency's two long-time media spokesmen, Denny Fleenor and Clarence Moriwaki.

In the spring of 2001, Earl announced the first of what would become several agency reorganizations. One of the goals, she wrote in a staff memo, was to "create an atmosphere where responsibility and accountability go hand in hand, allowing our employees opportunities to grow."

After outlining the changes, which included promoting Ahmad Fazel to director of Link, a move that would prove enormously important over time, she closed her memo with a few personal thoughts and a rah-rah for the beaten-down troops:

> Change can be invigorating, frightening, negative or positive depending on impact, attitude, and your personal choice to decide whether you will focus on making the changes work. I have no expectation that everyone will agree with or be happy with my decisions or even my process in reaching those decisions. It is my sincere request and hope that everyone chooses to make things work in ways that help us achieve our mission. Even if the headlines don't reflect our successes, we have much to be proud of...Our work is important, our products are desperately needed in this region and we have lots of opportunity to make a difference. Enthusiasm, attitude, passion and competence will get us there. Thanks for all you are doing on behalf of the citizens of this region.[7]

Not everyone thought Sound Transit had much to be proud of that spring. The *Seattle Times* editorial board, never a genuine supporter of Sound Transit, had seen enough. "Face Reality, Pull Plug on Light Rail" the headline read. "When big projects fail, this is how they die," the board wrote. "They develop wobbles and leaks. They are delayed. Plans are changed. Costs go up. Employees begin to bail out. Finally, long after everyone else knew it was over, some committee braves the embarrassment and pulls the plug."[8]

13

On the Firing Line

Joni had this baptism of fire on Capitol Hill.
—Peter Peyser

Joni Earl's upcoming testimony before Hal Roger's transportation subcommittee consumed her thinking for weeks, including what she would wear. In the last few days before flying to Washington, D.C., Earl and her husband, Charlie, took a long scheduled break to attend Seattle Mariners spring training in the Phoenix suburb of Peoria.

While Sound Transit was suffering through its worst spring ever, the Mariners were in Peoria exercising equal parts optimism and resignation. Gone from their roster and now playing for other teams were superstars Randy Johnson, Ken Griffey Jr., and Alex Rodriguez. What hope they had hinged on a Japanese legend looking to bring his maniacal focus and magical baseball skills to the American major leagues. In Japan Ichiro Suzuki had thunder in his bat and a cannon for an arm. He once had 210 hits in a season that was only 130 games long. The next year, although only five foot nine inches tall and a whippet-like 160 pounds, he muscled out 25 home runs. But now several weeks into spring training the Mariners' fiery manager Lou Piniella was anxious to see how Ichiro's skills would translate at baseball's highest level. So far Piniella wasn't impressed, wondering when the great hitter from Japan would display his power. It wasn't until the end of March that Ichiro would hit his first spring training home run. The Mariners looked so inept that Piniella called a special team meeting to vent his frustration. Players, he fumed, were missing signs, missing cutoffs, throwing to the wrong bases, and their playing was lackadaisical.[1] Piniella detested lackadaisical.

While the Mariners were working out their winter kinks in the Arizona sunshine, Mariners fan Joni Earl was obsessed with her upcoming subcommittee hearing. Included in her luggage were three fat briefing books stuffed with pie charts and weedy details about Link light rail. While others around her at the hotel pool read potboiler novels or snoozed in the desert heat, Earl was like a grad student cramming for finals. Every so often she would pause long enough to call Seattle for more information.

Earl felt enormous pressure. It was her first time testifying under oath on Capitol Hill and her mission was simple yet incredibly challenging: explain to a skeptical congressional committee what went wrong, why, and then how the agency was going to rebuild its credibility and actually get light rail built. She had been acting executive director for only two months, a Sound Transit employee all of five months, and yet on her shoulders rested the future of light rail in Seattle.

Earl once asked Sheila Dezarn, government affairs manager, the simple question that had such a complicated answer. "How did we get here?" Dezarn replied it was like an Agatha Christie mystery. "There's so many fingerprints on the knife, you'll never figure it out."

It was true, Earl would later agree. There was blame enough for all to share.

The D.C. hearing would take place in a small congressional committee room with just enough chairs for staff, a few lobbyists, and a couple of Seattle newspaper reporters. There would be no theatrics at this hearing, no Hollywood-style drama, yet for Earl the tension was as real as anything she'd ever experienced.

Years earlier, before she was an accomplished public speaker, Earl would blush brightly whenever nerves took over in front of an audience. The advice she received from a speaking instructor at the time was to wear red and avoid white, which would accentuate her blushing. For this trial on a national stage, Earl chose a red dress. "I figured I'd be blushing a lot," she said. "Oh god was I nervous."

• • •

Peter Peyser, one of Sound Transit's Capitol Hill lobbyists, was in the hearing room watching that afternoon. Testifying before Congress is daunting, he said, no matter what your experience or professional standing. "You're really on the firing line," he said.

Earl walked into that line of fire accompanied by Congressman Norm Dicks, who had already served more than two decades in Congress from a district that included Earl's hometown of Bremerton. Dicks was a whirlwind of action and a great proponent of Sound Transit and its mission of providing new transit options in the car-congested Puget Sound region. Not only did he walk in with Earl, he pointedly sat beside her at the table facing his congressional colleagues, some of them longtime friends.

Ric Ilgenfritz, Sound Transit's communications director, knew that Norm Dicks' gesture had great significance. It meant the congressman had Earl's back. "That's pretty old school," Ilgenfritz said. "He was one of the top two or three Democrats on that committee. Him sitting there tells Hal Rogers that if you mess with her you're messing with me. I'm going to stand here in public with her and support her while she explains what went wrong. It just gave Joni credibility."

As Earl and Dicks settled into their chairs, back in Seattle a group of Sound Transit staffers huddled around a computer listening to a live internet audio feed.

Earlier in the day, Roger's committee had questioned Hiram Walker, the FTA's Acting Deputy Administrator, and it was clear this hearing would be no love fest. Rogers roasted the FTA for what he considered its lack of oversight in awarding Sound Transit's $500 million grant. "That action is unconscionable and will not be tolerated," Rogers said.[2]

Later he would scold Walker: "Now you know that we are not going to do another (Boston) Big Dig don't you?"

"I do know that Mr. Chairman," Walker said. "I do not intend to participate in a Big Dig in Seattle."

Boston. Big. Dig. In early 2001, those three words sent leaders of the nation's largest public works projects diving for cover.

The job of replacing downtown Boston's elevated Interstate-93 with an underground highway took budget-busting to spectacular heights. Or lows. Besides building an underground highway, the Big Dig included new bridges over the Charles River, the extension of Interstate-90 to Logan International Airport, and the creation of Route 1A connecting downtown to the waterfront. The estimated price tag of $2.4 billion was laughably low with the final bill soaring over $14 billion, making it the most expensive highway project in the nation.

The federal government was initially on the hook for 90 percent, but after costs grew from exorbitant to ridiculous Congress capped its contribution, staunching the federal taxpayer bleeding. Massachusetts taxpayers were left with the balance.

The Boston experience had the effect of giving big public works plans, particularly those relying on federal dollars, a radioactive glow. Now the feds were much more apt to scrutinize every line in every budget.

• • •

Eventually, with the preliminaries brushed aside, Earl took her turn at the table and in a confident voice, presented an opening statement. "This is a very complicated and controversial project," she began. "I accept responsibility for the mistakes of the agency at this point in time."

But, she added, with solid oversight and assistance the agency was correcting those mistakes.

Then Earl sounded a theme she hoped would carry the day: "At the same time, we need to move forward."

Rogers spent several uncomfortable minutes hammering on a recently published *Seattle P-I* newspaper story that described 130 possible contaminated sites along the Link route (dramatically overblown as it turned out) as well as detailed questions about Link's schedule and financing. "Let me ask it bluntly," Rogers said. "Can you guarantee us that the total cost is not going to exceed $4.16 billion?"

"I cannot guarantee that," Earl replied. "I do believe they are not going up because of the way we have built the budget this time, but I cannot guarantee that."

Eventually, over several long minutes, the ice in the room began melting.

"There is a story that quotes you as saying you expect this hearing to be one of your less pleasant growth experiences," Rogers said.

"I was really sorry that that quote came in, Mr. Chairman," Earl said.

"We are hurt," the Kentucky congressman replied.

"It was really nothing personal," Earl said.

Congressman Dicks jumped in. "Your reputation precedes you, Mr. Chairman," he said.

"Well, you see we are not quite as bad as we seem," Rogers replied.

"Thank you, I appreciate that," Earl said.

"Like Mark Twain's comment about Wagner's music," Rogers said. 'It is not really as bad as it sounds.'"

After many more minutes of give and take, the hearing eventually wound down, but not without a last lecture for the visitor from Seattle. Congressman Rogers said:

> We don't want to get involved in local politics. We don't want to try to insert our judgment on what the community wants to do or not do. That is entirely the community's decision. What we are here to try to do is oversee expenditures of federal dollars...so I don't want anyone to get the idea that we are attempting to change or modify or torpedo or promote or anything else. We like to look out for the expenditure of taxpayer dollars. I hope you appreciate that on practically every project that gets this far along we hear nothing but good things about the project, and I hope you appreciate that we are getting a lot of mixed signals from Seattle about whether to proceed and, if so, how. So, we are a little confused about all of that... I hope you appreciate where we are coming from, from our perspective.[3]

"Absolutely," Earl said.

• • •

The feeling as the committee members filed out of the hearing room was that Earl was more than up to the challenge and had presented herself and Sound Transit with confidence and poise, if not something more.

"I remember being blown away by the way she handled that hearing, you know the professionalism, forthrightness, willingness to take on the challenges," Peyser said. "And she gave Rogers a little bit of the sense that the people in charge of this project aren't people who are just trying to waste our money."

Sheila Dezarn, Sound Transit's Government Relations manager, who was instrumental in securing the federal grant, recalled Earl's performance that day. "I felt like she was really kind of signaling that 'I am the CEO, I am here to answer your questions, you can have confidence in me.' She looked amazing."

It was entirely appropriate that the committee required Earl to fly to Washington, D.C. and present herself before them, Ilgenfritz said. "They lit into her but we screwed up, it was fair game. You don't tell the government that the project is going to cost a certain amount and have them give you half a billion dollars and then have it turn out that it's going to cost a whole lot more and you're putting that federal investment in jeopardy. That's a huge fuckup."

Agency spokesman Geoff Stuckart, who was one of those listening to the internet feed in Seattle, was impressed with how well Earl did, how prepared and self-assured she seemed. He was also struck by the honesty on both sides of the table that day. "It didn't feel like anyone was trying to score political points or anything like that. It was a genuine oversight function and probably merited; it was probably the way the public process should work," he said. "We had a big problem and questions and they said you fix it. You're not happy to be there but like a person who lives in a democracy that's kind of what I want."

Earl did so well in D.C. that it was shocking when, less than three months later, the Sound Transit Board would struggle internally over whether or not she was qualified to permanently lead the agency.

14

A Strong Counterpunch

Going out every morning to pick up the newspaper
was like picking up a hand grenade.
—Ron Lewis

The turnaround, many inside Sound Transit believed, began in a most outrageous way. In 2001, Seattle still had two competitive metro newspapers with a combined weekday circulation of around 400,000. For the *Seattle Post-Intelligencer* and the *Seattle Times,* there was often no bigger fish in the pond than Sound Transit.

Thomas Shapley, a longtime reporter, columnist, and then *P-I* editorial board member said it was altogether natural—and right—that Sound Transit drew the hot glare of the press. "We're talking about a lot of money, we're talking about an issue essential to the prosperity and livability of the region, the ability to get around," he said. "We thought it was a big deal, an important deal. Anytime you have a lot of money you don't need Chicago-style corruption, but you're going to have some powerful players and some powerful issues and some maneuvering."

On Friday, May 4, *Seattle P-I* newspapers hit porches and newsstands with a front page, above-the-fold headline that screamed: "Rail Costs Concealed."

In that article, reporter Chris McGann wrote that the true costs of Link had been repeatedly and knowingly concealed from voters and bond investors, in effect creating securities fraud. McGann's article went on to say that Sound Transit deliberately omitted $350 million in contingency money to make the project more palatable to voters in 1996. Besides hinting at criminal activity, the article attempted to draw parallels between Seattle's light rail project and the $14 billion Big Dig in Boston, the poster child for huge public works projects gone wrong.[1]

So much for a casual Friday heading into the weekend.

The *P-I* story reverberated across the region. Was this the "silver bullet" that adversaries had long hoped would bring down the struggling agency? Emory Bundy, outspoken Sound Transit foe, was quoted as saying that it was nearly impossible to prove where Sound Transit's "incompetence" ended and where its "deliberate misrepresentation" might have begun.[2]

Anxiety swept through Sound Transit offices. Paul Matsuoka, who was quoted in the story, said his jaw dropped when he saw the headline. "In the public sector you must always be ready to hear people call you incompetent or shortsighted, but to be called out criminally was stunning," he said.

Being accused of securities fraud on the front page of a metro newspaper is every finance officers' nightmare, said Brian McCartan, then deputy finance director at the time.

"Flabbergasted" was how Desmond Brown, Sound Transit's legal counsel felt. "I was really taken aback by it because I knew that it was completely false. I knew that people here were not concealing numbers. I knew that it was just wrong."

The article felt like a personal attack on every board member and employee of the agency. And it spread well beyond the walls of Union Station. Bob White, former Sound Transit director was at his sister's house in Nebraska saying goodbye to his father who was dying of cancer when his phone rang. "I hate to pile on here," his wife began. "But you should know that there's an article in today's *Seattle P-I* that says you lied to the Sound Transit Board and there's fraud." At that moment White, in his understated way, said he felt awful.

The article and its allegations were a surprise to Earl, who had no hint the story was being written and was not so much as asked for comment prior to publication, an obvious journalistic requirement for a story of such magnitude. Earl was attending a conference in Washington, D.C., when her cell phone exploded. Busy in a meeting, she let the calls go to voice mail.

Meanwhile Anne Fennessy, Sound Transit's acting communications director, was on the phone to Gov. Gary Locke, who as King County Executive had been a Sound Transit Board member during the time of the alleged fraud. Fennessy had been communications director for former Gov. Mike Lowry and still had the phone number to the governor's chauffeured car. A sitting governor involved in securities fraud? She dialed the governor in his car, briefed him on how the agency planned to respond and cautioned him about answering Sound Transit questions in upcoming interviews.

Finally, during a break in her D.C. meeting Earl checked her voicemail. The calls were from Fennessy and she sounded frantic. "I have to talk to you, I have to talk to you," she kept repeating. When the two connected, Fennessy blurted out: "You can't believe what just happened. We have World War III headlines in the *P-I* accusing the board of securities fraud. And it's really bad, it's a bad, bad story."

Fennessy said she was going on the radio to try to staunch the bleeding. "I'm going to tell them it's not true," she said. "Get on a plane and get back here."

A sickening feeling came over Earl, who remembers wondering out loud "do we know it's not true?"

She was convinced the Sound Transit Board, which included Bob Drewel her former longtime boss, would not engage in securities fraud, but Earl had only been at Sound Transit six months and was still assessing her staff. Cut off from her office on the nearly 3,000-mile plane ride home, Earl kept thinking "Oh my god please don't be true."

Back in Seattle, the shock wore off and a team soon assembled to parse the story word by word. Besides Fennessy, that team included Matsuoka, Geoff Stuckart, and Ahmad Fazel, the acting Link light rail director.

Fazel remembers Fennessy telling him if they didn't get a retraction on the *P-I* story, and soon, "there is not going to be a Sound Transit."

She wasn't just using scary hyperbole. Fennessy was tuned into the local political and business currents and in the spring of 2001, even though Sounder and ST Express were making impressive gains, Sound Transit was losing the battle for hearts and minds. Anti-light rail sentiment was spreading unchecked. An inflammatory article accusing the agency of the basest form of corruption could be the tipping point and had to be disproved—thoroughly and quickly.

From his initial read-through and brief analysis with others, Fazel felt the story rang false. He was confident enough to predict to Fennessy that within the next few days the *P-I* would "eat their words."[3] He pulled Stuckart and others into his office and had them autopsy the story, line by line, for anything that contributed to a conclusion of fraud. For Fazel, the story seemed anchored around the comments of one Sound Transit consultant who had been quoted in the article. Fazel talked to the consultant who said his reported comments were taken out of context. The consultant signed a statement saying as much. At the same time, others began analyzing old emails and pulling apart boxes of files.

Eventually, Fazel was certain the agency could disprove everything in the story that hinted at fraud. The task now was putting the proof together and explaining it to the public in an understandable way. Fazel's team soon had a thick three-ring binder of information that factually discounted every accusation. An email was delivered to a long list of leaders saying the *P-I* story was untrue and the agency was asking for a correction.

Rick Cocker, Fennessy's partner in their public affairs firm, said the newspaper's decision not to allow Sound Transit to respond to the story before publication showed how vulnerable the *P-I* perceived the agency to be. In the long tradition of journalism in such high-profile reporting, the newspaper would come to the agency, describe the conclusion of its investigation, and then ask for comment as part of the story. Even a "no comment" would show a good faith attempt. "They thought you were so weak they could do this with no consequences," Cocker said.

Stuckart had a similar reaction. "You get the sense of how beleaguered we were when Chris McGann could write the story he did and that people would believe that the agency would do that and that he believed it and his editors believed it and the public believed it."

Out of the chaos of that Friday came a lesson that Earl learned and never forgot: It's called the strong counterpunch.

• • •

Early the next week, lugging copies of their three-ring evidence binder, a contingent that included Earl, Fazel, Fennessy, and Matsuoka squeezed into a Sound Transit agency car and sped off for the *P-I* offices at the opposite end of downtown.

Earlier that day, the group had formed its strategy for the meeting: they would respectfully present their evidence and then, before leaving, insist on a correction—something they knew newspapers were almost pathologically opposed to, particularly on big, splashy investigative pieces. Thinking about what she was up against, Earl was even more nervous than when she had walked into the Hal Rogers congressional hearing. After all, she said, Sound Transit was going to tell a major metropolitan newspaper that it was wrong and, as the old saying goes, you don't pick a fight with anyone who buys ink by the barrel.

The Sound Transit group was ushered into a conference room just off the *P-I*'s newsroom. Sitting opposite from them was the newspaper publisher, two or three top editors, and the reporter, Chris McGann. Introductions were made. Nobody smiled.

The meeting was cordial but strained, both sides making their case and neither backing down. As the minutes passed, Earl had the sense the stone-faced editors weren't buying what she was selling. Matsuoka also felt the tension. At one point there was a give-and-take over the facts and Earl pointedly reminded the newspaper managers that this was the kind of dialogue that should have occurred *before* the story was published.

The meeting ended when one of the editors abruptly shut his binder, thanked Sound Transit for the information and stood to go. But before he could reach the door, Fennessy had a final word. She told the journalists that the agency was giving them time to study the evidence. But, she warned, the clock was ticking. She told them the agency had already called a press conference where it would publicly rebut every line of the *P-I*'s story. The agency had invited all the region's radio and television stations as well as the newspapers: the *Seattle Times*, Associated Press, *Tacoma News Tribune*, *Everett Herald*, and *The Stranger*.

As they piled back into the car for the trip to Union Station, the contingent of top managers from Sound Transit were unsure of what the *P-I* editors would do. The consensus in the car was that it could go either way. At the very least they agreed it felt good to roll up their sleeves and fight back.

• • •

The next few days, with their facts airtight, Fazel and others met reporters from around the region and disproved the *P-I* story line by line. Tellingly, no other major outlet had done much with the story.

As the days passed, there was only silence from the *P-I*'s top offices. And yet the information in the three-ring binder had an impact inside the newspaper. Although he was not involved in the meetings or the story, Shapley said Sound Transit's three-ring binder was impressive. Even 16 years later and retired to an Eastern Washington ranch, he still had a copy of that three-ring binder.

"Oh my god I have never seen such an extensive, detailed taking down in my entire life," he said. "I've kept it as an example of if you think you're being reported on inaccurately and you've got the facts to back it up, man here's a way to rip somebody to the ground."

Finally, on a Wednesday five days after the securities fraud story had hit the street, Earl was walking back from a meeting at the King County Courthouse when she checked her phone messages. One was from the *P-I*. "Joni, this is Chris McGann. I wanted to get a quote from you for the correction we are running."

Later, when Stuckart burst into a meeting of top leaders with the news, the room erupted in cheers.

The next day, Thursday, May 10, an above-the-fold story on the *P-I* front page read: "A *Seattle Post-Intelligencer* story Friday asserting that Sound Transit concealed the true cost of building a light-rail line from voters and bond investors by leaving out hundreds of millions of dollars in contingency costs was incorrect."[4]

David McCumber, the paper's managing editor, was quoted, saying, "Friday's Sound Transit story did not meet the *Post-Intelligencer*'s standards for accuracy and fairness. We regret that, and we want to set the record straight."

Earl believed, and many others agreed, that the correction was a turning point for Sound Transit. Before then, the strategy had generally been to let incorrect information go unchallenged under the theory that soon enough it would drift from the public's consciousness. But that approach naïvely underestimated the collective effect of such stories. Earl said the *P-I* correction put the media on notice that "you're holding *us* accountable, now we're going to hold *you* accountable."

Finance Director Brian McCartan said the counterpunch became Earl's trademark and after that no charge was left unanswered. Multi-page rebuttals with clarifying facts became the standard. "Nobody gets away with a cheap shot," McCartan said. "She was ready for battle every day."

Shapley, the *P-I* newspaper veteran who later became senior director of public affairs for the Washington State Department of Social and Health Services, knows what it's like to work both inside and outside of government. He believes Sound Transit took the right approach in challenging the story. "It was the absolutely correct strategy because too many times, especially government, you take it because you're afraid to piss people off and you're afraid you're going to make an enemy, but you just have to step up. But boy, you better have it nailed."

Following the *Post-Intelligencer's* front page correction, Earl's stature within the organization grew. It was not only that she fought hard for the agency, it was that she fought hard to defend actions that took place years before she even came to Sound Transit.

Matsuoka felt his relationship with Earl had changed. Before they were at arm's length, a little wary of each other. When the *P-I* story hit she could have said "let's move on, I'm new here and I can't speak for sins of the prior administration." Just as easily, Matsuoka could have been thrown under the bus and blamed. "But after that, I knew she stood up for people," he said. "I knew she stood up for truth for what's right and that meant a lot to me personally."

It wasn't just opponents who were on notice. Staff knew when they were preparing a rebuttal or a report, they better be on their game. "She was not going to take a weak punch, she wasn't going to make a bad case for the agency," McCartan said.

Board member Greg Nickels said the board also felt the change. "There was a new attitude, a less defensive attitude, a more assertive attitude. As a board member out there getting shot at it felt good to have that behind you, that felt a lot stronger."

The events surrounding the retraction also had a profound effect on Fazel, who at that time was considering his future. With his strong reputation throughout the industry, he'd receive the occasional call from another project in another city, gauging his interest in leaving.

"I began telling people this is my project now," Fazel said. "I had a feeling Sound Transit would be successful and I wanted to continue."

• • •

The first thing many employees did every morning was check the local newspapers to see where the Sound Transit headline was going to be: on the front page top of the fold, the B Section top of the fold, or leading the editorial pages.

Newspaper editorial boards, whose job is to comment on issues, were eager to weigh in on anything Sound Transit, particularly its light rail program. Strong editorials not only influenced public opinion, they sometimes led lawmakers and government leaders to change direction. Thomas Shapley, the longtime *Seattle P-I* editorial board member, said the *P-I* board supported increased transit but wanted to make sure it was done right and that taxpayer dollars were spent wisely. "The most important thing was that we got transit that was legitimate, economical, successful and did the job," he said.

Earl once joked that she felt like throwing a party the first day there was no Sound Transit story in the newspaper, or on the radio or television news. If sorted into two piles, one positive, one negative, Sound Transit staffers surely felt the negative pile dwarfed the other. Turning around such aggressive media took relentless adherence to a plan.

Stuckart came to Sound Transit for his skill at "crisis communications," in other words putting a floor on the elevator drop of bad news. That was his specialty following years of working media for political campaigns.

Although still in his 20s, Stuckart had the maturity of someone much older and was adept at rebuilding relationships with reporters. He knew that reporters didn't trust the agency but, since he was new, he had the standing to tell them: "I'm going to be straight with you and…give you the facts and yes, I'm going to give you our perspective, but I'm not going to lie and I'm not going to hide stuff."

Ric Ilgenfritz was in the process of interviewing for Sound Transit's communications director job when the *P-I* story broke. He said the adversarial attitude of the press versus Sound Transit was brutal. But with Ilgenfritz in charge and with Stuckart, along with longtime Seattle radio reporter Lee Somerstein as agency spokesmen, Sound Transit was about to take the offensive.

"Joni was adamant about the importance of transparency and disclosure and so we were going to dare the media to find us at fault, to uncover more stuff," Ilgenfritz said. "We figured we had disclosed everything and we hit bottom and there was no other baggage to find so we were going to challenge them."

The result was that Sound Transit pressed the media for corrections every time it saw something even remotely inaccurate. The effect, Ilgenfritz said, was reporters started calling more often to fact check before publishing. Eventually, as relationships improved, reporters learned that what Sound Transit told them was true.

For the public and the press the result, starting with the *P-I* correction, was a different way of looking at Sound Transit. As Stuckart said, "we were not the bleeding fish in the ocean attracting sharks anymore. There wasn't blood in the water."

But the media scrutiny served a purpose. Shapley pointed out that the press was essential in highlighting the changes needed at Sound Transit. "Things don't get fixed until people know they need fixing and often the only way that happens is that somebody reports it," he said. "And when that happens you can either fold your arms and say 'no it doesn't need fixing' or 'let's fix it.' It's rare that institutions fix themselves. Somebody has to come along and hold up a mirror."

15

A Near Miss

Sometimes I think we should build a really tall statue to her.
—Desmond Brown

Joni Earl's Sound Transit career was very nearly over just eight months in.

By June 2001, the board was ready to replace Bob White, who had left in January. A national search ensued and then a special Sound Transit Board committee interviewed finalists before recommending a new director.

For many at Sound Transit, as well as the greater Puget Sound community, Earl seemed obvious. They would point out that in less than a year she had already unraveled the costs and timeline for building Link, set the agency on the path to achieve it, stared down Hal Rogers, rode out an earthquake, and forced the *Seattle P-I* to correct a story that would have crippled the agency. She knew the region's people and issues, morale inside Union Station was improving, and there was a feeling that Sound Transit was poised to go toe-to-toe with its critics.

Besides actually getting light rail construction up and running, what was left to prove? Finalists for the top job included the former director of the Los Angeles Metropolitan Transit Authority's rail program, the former director of the Oregon Department of Transportation, and a senior manager for the Massachusetts Bay Transportation Authority. And, of course, acting director Joni Earl.

Before any decisions were made, Earl asked the search committee that whatever its choice, they not announce it publicly because it would be embarrassing and unfair to the other candidates if the full board chose someone else.

Instead, after taking up the better part of a Saturday interviewing finalists and talking it over, the search committee announced its recommendation: Joni Earl. They shot out a press release saying as much and then scheduled the coronation for three days later.

And yet some on the Sound Transit Board weren't convinced of her qualifications and unbeknownst to Earl a showdown was brewing. Leading up to the selection, one of the agency's top directors was working behind the scenes trying to persuade board members not to hire Earl. What should have been a day of personal achievement and satisfaction would become the roughest she endured so far.

Television cameras were set up outside the boardroom at Union Station Tuesday, June 12, in anticipation of the announcement. The print press gathered as well. The first hint of trouble came early as Earl was walking downstairs and passed John Ladenburg, the new Pierce County Executive who had joined the board in January. Ladenburg would eventually become a favorite among Sound Transit staffers for his honest straightforward manner. A former Pierce County prosecutor, he once publicly shut down a particularly irritating and noisy critic, who happened to be a disgraced lawyer, by telling him during a meeting "the board won't be taking advice from a disbarred attorney." Plus, Ladenburg wore cowboy boots with his business suits.

As he passed her on the stairs, Ladenburg stopped Earl. "We're having a little bit of trouble here," he said.

"What do you mean?" she later recalled saying.

"We've got a board member who doesn't believe you meet the qualifications."

This, Earl said, was what she was afraid would happen when the committee made its recommendation public the Saturday before.

As Ladenburg continued up the steps Earl quickly sought out board member Bob Drewel, her old boss and longtime friend, who assured her there wasn't a problem. Shortly after, the board went into its scheduled 25-minute, closed-door meeting. Earl waited outside. But now she had reason to worry about what was happening inside those closed doors.

• • •

Board Chair Dave Earling quickly discovered that not everyone in the meeting room shared his enthusiasm for Joni Earl. For him, it was enthusiasm born in trust. Over the years, starting in Snohomish County, Earling, Earl, and Drewel had developed an unshakeable partnership they frequently relied upon when they began working together on the region's mass transit project.

But this early on in the project, not everyone on the board had the same confidence in her. A surprisingly large group of board members argued that Sound Transit needed a high-profile, internationally-known light rail expert who, they believed, would restore the agency's credibility. Earling understood their reasoning, but countered that the agency would be better served by someone well-schooled in internal agency structures and, more importantly, was already well respected throughout the region. That leader, he said, was acting director Joni Earl.

Leading the opposition was Kevin Phelps, a Tacoma councilmember and businessman who was new to the Sound Transit Board. Phelps preached fiscal discipline with a reformist's uncompromising zeal. He wanted a national leader to run the organization and was unhappy that not all board members were included in the interview and selection process.[1]

State Transportation Secretary Doug MacDonald, another outspoken board member, characterized the conflict inside the room as "nuances of enthusiasm" for choosing someone other than Earl.[2]

There was also a slight undercurrent of concern that Earl, who had been Snohomish County's longtime second in charge under county executive Bob Drewel, was "Drewel's guy" and as such more interested in county matters than transit issues.

"And so yeah, there were questions," said Greg Nickels, who that summer was involved in a heated campaign for Seattle mayor and was desperate for Sound Transit to succeed. When Earl was hired as chief operating officer, Nickels told her in plain language that he was disappointed in the hire because she lacked transit experience. Now, eight months later, he recognized her worth.

"I thought she'd won our confidence, so even though she wasn't a transit guy, she was our guy. I think loyalty is real important and I know she was loyal to Bob but that did not stop her from being absolutely loyal to the board and to the agency as a whole. There was never a point where you thought she was running Bob Drewel's agenda as opposed to the Sound Transit Board's agenda."

Inside the meeting room the temperature was rising.

As talk continued about a national search and national transit experts, Drewel finally ran out of patience. "Bullshit, you need somebody who can run an organization and is capable of learning about transit," he remembers telling his fellow board members. "You *will not* find anybody as capable as Joni Earl."

More often than not, it was Drewel who the Sound Transit Board sent to Washington, D.C., to lobby FTA leaders and the state's congressional delegation. "Face work in D.C." as Drewel called it. Now he rose from his chair to address his fellow board members. "Don't ever ask me to go back to Washington, D.C., to explain to Patty Murray and Norm Dicks why we didn't hire Joni Earl!" he said.

But then another issue emerged. Earl later learned that one of her top directors had told a board member that if Earl was chosen as permanent director, staff would quit in protest.

With both sides thus locked, the 25-minute meeting stretched to an hour with no end in sight.

Eventually Earling, chair of the board, stood and said he was going to go out and get Joni for some answers. Others talked him out of it and he sat back down as the discussion continued.

• • •

Earl was still waiting outside the meeting room when the board took a break. Several of them walked by and to her they looked as if they'd "been through a ringer." She approached Earling. "Is everything ok?"

"No."

She asked if she was going to be invited in to talk to the board.

"I don't know," he said and turned away. "I've got to go."

Earl thought, what the hell is going on in there?

Eventually she left her place outside the board room and found a vacant office in the basement of Union Station where she grew increasingly anxious. She was joined by Ric Ilgenfritz, the recently hired communications director, who tried to calm her. Ilgenfritz himself had a huge stake in the proceedings—a clause in his employment agreement allowed him a severance if the board did not retain Earl and he was prepared to use it. "I wasn't going to stay if Joni wasn't going to stay," he would later say. Now he tried to reassure his boss. "It's going to be fine, it's going to be fine. The board will get to the right place and what matters is the staff and everyone here is behind you and ready to go." But were they?

As the wait stretched on, she grew increasingly angry and there was nothing Ilgenfritz could say to ease her mind.

• • •

The television cameras had packed up and left and most of the reporters had wandered away.

Finally, two hours into their 25-minute meeting Drewel, who was sitting beside Ladenburg, remembers saying to him: "John, you have to stop this."

Ladenburg agreed and told the board they had to make a decision, and needed to move forward. As Earling recalled, Ladenburg became the swing vote to approve Earl. That did it. The board then agreed to make it unanimous. As they waited for Earl to join them in open public session for the official vote, Phelps slipped out and was in his car heading back to Tacoma. If he had stayed, Phelps would have voted no.[3]

"It was a very hard meeting, hard not only on the board because we got pretty direct but also for Joni because it took so long," Earling said.

As the board waited for her, Earl was nowhere to be found. Earling and Drewel went out to track her down.

She was still in that basement meeting room and by now was furious. After months of working 18-hour days, of spending weekends inside her corner office in Union Station instead of on her boat with her husband, Charlie, and of taking blows for the agency in public and behind closed doors, she felt that the board's reluctance was a public rebuke of her credibility.

Ilgenfritz left the room to the two board members who were Earl's longtime associates and friends. All three had been leaders together in Snohomish County and had attended countless meetings and events over the years. They convinced her to come upstairs to the board meeting for the official vote.

Earl would never forget walking through the board room doors. "They invited me in and I didn't know what to expect and Dave [Earling] said 'I have a motion will somebody move,' and it got a second and then he said 'all in favor' and that was it. They didn't say anything about my qualifications, they didn't say anything positive, that was just it."

Afterwards, she had another private meeting with Earling and Drewel. "I was livid and I told them I don't want your fucking job."

Drewel and Earling stayed with her as she worked the anger out of her system. Drewel missed his scheduled flight that night to Chicago.

• • •

The *Seattle Times* editorial board took Earl's hiring as another opportunity to publicly bash Sound Transit:

> Sound Transit is gasping on life support because its mission and credibility are in tatters. The once bright promise of a light rail line that would grow to complement other regional transportation projects is in near ruins. A national search brought before the board a talent list rich with management and engineering experience on some of the biggest public works projects in the United States. It was a great list of finalists. Yet, when it came down to a crucial choice, all the outsider candidates were blithely ignored....Did the board not comprehend the requirement for fresh ideas unconnected to the agency's past? Was there no larger vision to find a new executive director to signal a fresh slate and a fresh start? The size of the agency's challenge to redeem light rail, and the scale of its failure to deliver, have not yet hit home with the board.[4]

The events of that day served as motivation for Earl. As Ilgenfritz would later point out, you underestimated Joni Earl at your own peril. That was true for the agency as well. "If she felt like she was being questioned, she wasn't being accorded the respect and courtesy she felt the agency deserved, she would rise to that in a very determined way and assert the agency's prerogatives," he said. The reluctance of some on the board to hire Earl as director seemed a challenge to her credibility, which was one of her core leadership values. As her father in Bremerton had told her, the only real currency in life is your word, your credibility.

It wasn't long before that difficult day became just a footnote in Joni Earl's long career at Sound Transit, and everyone would look back at it with a mystified "what were they thinking?" The agency director who had worked against her hiring quit about six weeks later. There were no other staff defections.

Earl later summed the day up by saying, simply: "It worked out in the end."

16

Hard Pivot South

I hope nobody else has to go through this.
—Ahmad Fazel

As the Joni Earl era began at Sound Transit, another leader got his chance as well.

Ahmad Fazel was born in Iran and as a young man came to the United States to study engineering at Washington State University. By the time he reached Sound Transit in the year 2000, he had already enjoyed a productive career on light rail projects across the West. Fazel had been project director of planning and development for Denver's Regional Transportation District, which opened two light rail corridors on time and under budget. He was also systems engineer for Portland's Tri-Met Westside light rail project.

As he looked around and took stock of his new agency in Seattle, Fazel was puzzled by the number of consultants working on the light rail project. In Denver, most light rail engineering took place in-house. Sound Transit, by contrast, was structured to manage consultants, who did most of the actual engineering. Fazel was also struck by how the agency seemed to have a knack for making solvable problems overwhelming.

"It doesn't have to be this complicated," Fazel recalled thinking. "Simplify it."

Despite his success elsewhere, Fazel found himself buried deep in the Sound Transit organizational chart. From his vantage point looking up he saw opportunities for improvements but to his growing dissatisfaction he wasn't even invited to the important meetings where such discussions took place. About that time he began updating his resume, wondering "what the hell did I do" moving to Seattle.

Fortunately his prospects improved considerably when Lyndon "Tuck" Wilson, acting Link director after Paul Bay left, unexpectedly recommended Fazel as his deputy director. Wilson, whose open-door policy extended to actually having the door to his office removed, had worked with Fazel in Portland. Wilson made enquiries about Fazel's time in Denver and learned he had successfully steered that project through similar difficulties.

When he interviewed with Earl for the Link deputy job, Fazel told her he "didn't want to be the guy just doing performance evaluations." He convinced her that going forward, the agency could benefit from his experience and ideas. Before long he was not only deputy Link director, he was helping form strategy at the agency's highest level.

• • •

Sound Transit took another hit in June 2001 when Tuck Wilson announced he was quitting his temporary Link directorship and heading back to Portland. Before leaving he had a chat with Earl about the future direction of the light rail department. Surprisingly to Earl, he recommended Fazel as his replacement.

"I credit Tuck because he said you have a guy and he is really good and should be acting director," Earl recalled. She brought Fazel into her office for a long talk after which she offered the temporary leadership job to a man who was mostly unknown. "I think there were a lot of people who were befuddled by the whole thing," she said.

Light rail in Seattle was about to change. As the new acting Link director, Fazel told Earl to expect his approach to be very different. "I'm not going to blow this thing up and put committees together," he said. "I will just do it." He reminded Earl that the agency was spending some $15 million to $20 million a month in Link consultants. "I said we need to stop that and she said 'go for it.'" He started working with the agency's attorneys and contracts department to, as he said, "stop the bleeding."

"I told Joni we have nothing to be ashamed of, voters approved this and we are making it reality," Fazel said. "We are not the team that created the problem, we are the team that's going to solve this problem."

When the opportunity arose months later to apply for the permanent Link directorship, Fazel initially demurred. "I thought Joni would want to hire somebody external, somebody with a bigger profile, I had no expectations to become the director," he said. "I thought the politics of the board was they wanted name recognition, some guy nationally known, not some guy with an accent."

But by then he had impressed powerful board members, including Ron Sims and Greg Nickels, and eventually he was persuaded to at least apply. Thinking he had little chance for the job, Fazel was fully at ease during his interview with Earl and Vernon Stoner, Sound Transit's deputy director.

A few weeks later Joni Earl stopped by his office. "Ahmad, you're the director," she said.

• • •

In the best organizations, particularly complex ones with many moving parts, the trust between executive director and top managers is unequivocal and mutual. In that regard, the working relationship between Earl and Fazel blossomed.

"Ahmad was so good," Earl would later say. "Ahmad was why we got the system open and operating, he was so disciplined and focused. When he gave me July 2009 [for opening light rail] he said 'I promise you we will make this date, I give you my word, don't worry about this date.' Boy, he lived up to it."

For her part, Earl backed Fazel when others in the agency took exception to his aggressive style. "In some divisions and departments I wasn't very popular," Fazel said. "A lot of people would go to her office and complain about my approach, but I said to Joni when you're building a project like this you can't always have consensus internally, you need to make decisions and move forward." As he was starting out, Fazel told Earl: "I need your support because people from contracts and legal and other departments will come to you and complain and say what the hell is this guy doing?"

Fazel said Earl's support was critical. She hired good people, trusted them and let them do their job.

While Earl believed in her staff and didn't meddle in the day-to-day, there was little in the agency she didn't know. Desmond Brown, Sound Transit's legal counsel, marveled at her ability to grasp and retain details. "I have seen Joni Earl talking in detail and in very intelligent fashion the merits of various types of coatings that you put on screws. I told her you shouldn't know this, you should not be sitting there at midnight reading reports on this," he said. "I've never been in a meeting with her when she had to rely on anyone else for any detail. She knew it and that meant that she could ask the right questions to get the issues resolved and get the information necessary."

Daphne Cross, Earl's longtime senior executive assistant who became one of her closest friends, had a front room window into Earl's working style. Cross would often emerge from a meeting amazed at Earl's appetite for facts. "She would say in a meeting we should use a one and a quarter-inch tie instead of a two-inch tie because it has more give. People in the meeting would look at her like: 'why do you know that?'"[1]

That knowledge wasn't just for show, it gave her and the agency an advantage in tough negotiations. Those who expected to steamroll the thin, blonde woman in the corner office, soon learned otherwise.

Time and again Cross would watch important people, often oozing arrogance, walk into Earl's office as if the varsity had just arrived in town. "After that first meeting, they didn't underestimate her anymore."

• • •

Brian McCartan remembers one of his first meetings with Earl. It was before a board meeting when he and then CFO Hugh Simpson huddled with her to talk strategy.

"We were explaining the numbers to her and we were talking each other into, well, if we do this this could happen and if we do this that could happen. We were making it really complicated, like we were anticipating how everyone would come at us. She said 'Ok, you guys have made this way too hard. I'm going to go in there and tell them what the number is and let the chips fall from there.'"

It was, he said, startling and fresh and totally the correct way to operate.

That new way of thinking was beginning to wash through Sound Transit. In such a way early in 2001 the agency took a hard pivot and decided instead of immediately trying to figure out how to deep tunnel under First Hill and Capitol Hill to the UW, it would first consider going the less expensive, less challenging route south from downtown, through the Rainier Valley and then to the airport. But because the south leg would carry far fewer riders, the north-south switch would require soul-searching, months of study, and of course, the inevitable howling from critics.

Paul Schell, Seattle mayor and Sound Transit Board member, raised the south-first idea in a letter to an independent outside committee that was studying the light rail project. About two weeks later, following some serious number crunching, Sound Transit announced that it could not build the entire 21-mile line from SeaTac to the UW by the year 2009—it was at least $190 million short. "We're going to have to change the alignment," declared board member Ron Sims.[2]

Going south would free up more time to study the project's more challenging and costly north segment. But the south route had its own basket of problems, starting with the assumption the agency could untangle its issues with the U.S. Inspector General, amend its federal grant application to the FTA, and then actually receive its $500 million grant.

Another problem was that the Port of Seattle, which operated Sea-Tac Airport, was not ready with its plans to bring light rail into the airport. The Port's delay meant that for a while the southern terminus would be the Tukwila International Blvd Station, 1.7 miles from the airport, or about a four-minute shuttle bus ride away. A light rail line that couldn't even connect to the airport seemed glaringly incomplete. Opponents pounced, dubbing it "the train to nowhere."

Board member Rob McKenna, who was vice chair of the Sound Transit Finance Committee, was typically blunt: "My prediction is that by the time we get this thing built or even under construction, Seattle is going to decide it wants to go with the monorail."[3]

About that time a Seattle woman wondered if a bake sale could raise enough money to get light rail to the airport. "I'd hold a series of bake sales if that's what's needed," Sharon Griggins joked to a *Seattle P-I* reporter. Desmond Brown, Sound Transit's general counsel, played along: "There is no limit on gifts or grants. In fact, that is specifically stated in the enabling legislation," he told the *P-I*.[4]

Few others found humor in the go-south decision. Ted Van Dyk, a columnist for the *Seattle P-I* whose general crankiness was often directed at Sound Transit, wrote that area taxpayers, citizens, business owners, and commuters were justified in marching "with torches and pitchforks" to the doorsteps of Sound Transit Board members.

"In less tolerant and easy-going states like ours, mad-as-hell transportation users and taxpayers already would have filed lawsuits and recall petitions against the Sound Transit Boardmembers," he grumbled.[5]

Despite Van Dyk's call, no board member ever reported pitchforks and torches at their doorsteps.

Still another problem was that running light rail through Seattle also meant sharing the Downtown Seattle Transit Tunnel with buses. King County Metro built and opened the 1.3-mile tunnel in 1990 to eventually handle light rail, but mainly to keep buses off busy downtown streets. Running buses and trains together in the tunnel would take a choreography seldom seen between transit systems. Sound Transit, feeling pressure from business and city leaders, was reluctant to kick buses out of the tunnel for trains. Following negotiations that became testy at times, both agencies signed on to a plan they called joint operations. Seattle would become one of the few places in the world where transit trains and buses shared a tunnel. The negotiations also determined that once trains were running, King County Metro would operate them.

Fazel remembers Sound Transit's safety manager saying in a meeting that it would be dangerous running buses and trains together in the tunnel. Afterwards, Fazel pulled him aside and said: "I heard you just bought a house, are you planning to sell it and move out of town?" The safety manager, with a puzzled look, wondered why Fazel would ask such a question. "Because," Fazel said, "if there's not going to be joint operations in the tunnel, there's not going to be a project."

Fazel agreed that starting south was a good idea and pursued it with vigor. "I said we need to have a story of how we're going to build this project. We need to give this region hope." He also realized that the agency had to get going on light rail or risk losing its technical team. Lost time inevitably leads to brain drain as light rail experts begin drifting away to other projects in other cities. Losing your technical capacity, Fazel knew, is a terrible blow to morale and to maintaining schedules.

Already the engineers below him were growing restless. Henry Cody, one of the top managers in the department, was frustrated by the inaction. "You can't study the geology forever" was his common refrain. "Why can't we get this thing going?"

The official green light to start south took the better part of 2001, although about halfway through the year the conclusion seemed foregone. The agency called it the initial segment, or first leg, and announced that the 14-mile $2.1 billion line would open by 2009.

Brian McCartan said the decision to go south felt like a make or break moment for the young agency. "I remember thinking this is maybe the stupidest move or the smartest thing we ever did. But I knew that the agency had cast the die."

• • •

When Sound Transit announced that it would build south first but trains wouldn't be running until 2009, someone asked Fazel the inevitable question: "Can you do it any sooner?"

"We can't do miracles," he remembers replying.

The only miracle in a light rail project is when the first passenger actually climbs on board and trains begin running for real.

As Fazel knew, building light rail is a slow, plodding process of planning, buying property, meetings, more meetings, engineering, construction, and testing. And then more meetings. Years of planning and station design are required before the hard hats arrive. In Seattle, community leaders, cities, elected officials, and neighborhoods were given every opportunity to weigh in. Planning also had to account for the area's unique local challenges that include steep hills, bodies of water, dense inner core neighborhoods, glacial soils that make tunneling difficult, and the region's love of process.

The actual construction of a light rail project typically lasts five years or longer and even at that unexpected delays can arise anytime. Link crews digging by the Duwamish River near Tukwila, for instance, unearthed hundreds of Indian artifacts, including tools that were at least 250 years old. Later, work stopped during construction near downtown Seattle when shoes, bits of furniture, dishes, and the top of a Rainier beer bottle from the late 1800s were uncovered and carefully preserved.

Especially complex or challenging projects, such as those requiring tunneling, can take seven years or more. Finally, the last six months to a year in the lifecycle of a light rail project is devoted to testing to make sure that operators are trained and that all communications, signals, crossing gates, and other systems will function under the stress of day-to-day operations.

Thus a light rail line, if all goes as planned start to finish, can take a decade or longer to build.

Link, of course, did not go as planned.

17

The Daily Slog

Now it's time to get on with it.—Joni Earl

For Joni Earl, still working inhuman hours, there was little time for anything outside Sound Transit. Occasionally she made it across the street to Safeco Field, home of her Seattle Mariners, who were shockingly, amazingly, putting together a summer for the ages. In his first months on the job, Ichiro Suzuki was baffling American League pitchers with his magical black-stained bat.

Never had a year seemed brighter for baseball in Seattle. Light rail was another matter as Earl spent the remainder of 2001 searching for Sound Transit's lost credibility.

The road was long and occasionally meandering but she knew that credibility would only be found in the daily slog of good work. Like the Mariners winning day after day with a focus on the long haul, Earl knew that small victories would someday add up to a bigger picture of success. Or at least that was her hope.

The ever-observant Ron Lewis, who was moving up the ranks in the light rail department and would one day be its executive director, saw how it would unfold. "The rebirth would come from the inside out," he said. "People at the core of the agency knew there was light at the end of the tunnel, we knew that we could reset it on the inside but then you've got to broaden that to the public."

While that reset worked its way inside out, the day-to-day running of Sound Transit in the summer of 2001 was punctuated by other, sometimes flashier, news that kept the agency in the public spotlight. On a slow news day, Sound Transit was always good for a headline.

July was a particularly busy month. The Sound Transit Board officially terminated its contract with Modern Transit Constructors, the firm selected a year earlier to design and build the light rail tunnel from downtown to the University of Washington. With the emphasis now on first laying tracks south, there was no immediate need for the northbound tunnel. Sound Transit paid Modern Transit Constructors a $900,000 honorarium for its time and efforts.

Later that month Paul Price, the director of Sounder commuter rail, left the agency and returned to San Diego. Price was the third major departure in less than a year following Executive Director Bob White and Link Director Paul Bay. His leaving caused a minor ripple in the press.

Also in July, a federal judge ruled on a lawsuit brought by the Rainier Valley opposition group, Save Our Valley, who were fighting for light rail in a tunnel rather than street level through their neighborhoods. Their lawsuit claimed that in planning Link through the Rainier Valley, Sound Transit violated federal environmental, housing, and civil rights laws. Ironically, many years earlier when light rail was first proposed in a tunnel under the valley, many residents living there demanded that it run on surface streets anticipating the economic development it would bring. No one would admit to feeling that now.

The grassroots Save Our Valley group was energetic and far-reaching and it seemed that every other yard or storefront window on Martin Luther King Jr. Way had a Save Our Valley sign. Their lawsuit, if successful, would have immediate and dramatic effect because by building light rail south the Rainier Valley was one of the first areas scheduled for construction. Tunneling would have added between $400 and $600 million to the project's price tag, making it far beyond reach.

So with great anxiety both sides awaited the ruling from U.S. District Court Judge Barbara Rothstein. On July 15 when she announced her decision to dismiss the suit, there were relieved smiles throughout Union Station. Another hurdle to Link construction was eliminated.

About a month later, to shift attention from its light rail project, the agency tried drumming up news coverage for two minor ridership achievements. The first was honoring the half millionth Sounder commuter train rider. Scott Conrad, a 35-year-old research technician from Puyallup, was randomly chosen as he stepped off a Sounder train on his way to work one morning at King Street Station. He was photographed, presented with a certificate and framed poster of a Sounder train and then sent on his way, surely befuddled by what just happened. Celebrating 500,000 riders must have seemed contrived to other commuter rail systems across the nation that routinely carry millions every year.

The second event was a press release announcing that Sound Transit's two-year old ST Express bus service had broken the 10 million mark for ridership. Earl and other top agency leaders took morning breaks at three park-and-ride lots to thank riders, who most likely wondered why the smiling director of a transit agency was handing them coffee.

Agnes Govern, director of the ST Express bus department, recalled that with so much attention on light rail, buses were almost an afterthought.

"Nobody cared about buses," she said. "In some ways for us that was really good because we could keep our heads down and focus in other ways. It had to help the agency in some way too, because you could at least point to projects being delivered and service actually happening."

To underscore that point, two new ST Express bus routes began running in late summer 2001, one serving East King County, the other Pierce County.

But when image-burnishing efforts like celebrating 10 million bus rides fell short, Earl felt the need to give public perception a not-so-gentle nudge. In August, she penned a column in the *Seattle Times* entitled "Sound Transit's Ready: Let's Get on with It":

> I know that Sound Transit is under the public microscope—and deservedly so—but, I have a message for our critics and our supporters. We have the know-how, we have the resources and we have strong public demand for action. Now it's time to get on with it. While an open and honest public debate is critical to our success, there comes a time to stop digging through the past and raise our eyes to the future. When I do that I see a bright future for Sound Transit and the region.[1]

Despite Earl's public optimism that the agency's credibility was returning, if ever so slowly, scrutiny was still red-hot. Deep down she knew there was a long way to go.

• • •

Also making headlines that summer and early fall was the contentious race for Seattle mayor which, true to form in 2001, became another forum to debate Sound Transit and the future of light rail in the region.

Greg Nickels, who had been fighting for light rail practically since high school, was in the race for his political life. Nickels' opponent was Seattle City Attorney Mark Sidran, a Harvard-educated lawyer who grew up in Seattle, but whose edgy style was similar to that of New York Mayor Rudy Giuliani. Sidran never missed an opportunity to blame Nickels for Sound Transit's delays and credibility problems.[2] "In a very direct way, this mayoral election is a referendum on Sound Transit," Sidran said.[3] One of his television ads showed a traffic jam with two women speaking in the background. One of the voices called Sound Transit the worst tax sinkhole in history.

Nickels remembered being constantly on the defensive about Sound Transit. "The thing I got hit with in the mayor's race was, you haven't laid an inch of rail, it's been five years and you haven't laid an inch of rail and you haven't broken ground," he said. "We needed some wins, some visible wins to help rebuild that confidence."

Bruce Ramsey, the *Seattle Times* editorial columnist and longtime Sound Transit cynic, wasn't about to give Nickels a break. "This is the election about light rail," he wrote. "It is not on the ballot, because it is not in the interest of the evangelists of rail and the paid providers of rail to put it on the ballot. But it is there.... There is still time to prevent this embarrassment. It's time to kill it, and get serious about things that will actually work: buses, vans, carpools and—dare we say it?—roads."[4]

• • •

September 11, 2001, began as any other working Tuesday. The Puget Sound forecast was 75 degrees and sunny, one of summer's last payoffs before the inevitable months of drizzle.

Teri Bubnick, whose job was making sure Sound Transit's mail and copy center in the basement of Union Station hummed smoothly, climbed on a Sounder train in Auburn that morning and joined hundreds of other sleepy commuters on their way into Seattle. Around her fellow passengers dozed or glanced through their newspapers reading items that within minutes would seem laughably trivial: the Seattle City Council spending $638,000 a year on five high-end self-cleaning public toilets; King County unveiling the sites for its new sewage treatment plan; Ichiro getting another hit as the Mariners won their

104th game of the year. The world seemed an ordinary place that morning for those commuters into Seattle.

Then all at once cell phones in purses and pockets throughout the train exploded to life. From the seats around her Bubnick heard: "Oh my god, oh my god!" Before long everyone on that Sounder train knew about the 9-11 terrorist attacks in New York City and Washington, D.C. Most mornings Bubnick saw tired or getting-ready-for-work faces, today she saw fear and disbelief. The rest of the ride into Seattle, she said, was surreal.[5]

Like others across the country, many of the passengers on Sounder trains or ST Express buses wondered if they were next. Although thousands of miles from the attacks, the West Coast seemed vulnerable. Less than two years earlier the Puget Sound region was put on edge when Ahmed Ressam, later dubbed the Millennium Bomber, was stopped in Port Angeles while trying to enter the United States from Canada. In his spare wheel well were 10 green plastic garbage bags filled with 118 pounds of a white power used to manufacture explosives. Ressam was part of a plot to bomb the Los Angeles International Airport on the eve of the new millennium.

In September 2001 most of Sound Transit's Union Station was not yet wired for cable television and desk computers couldn't stream video, so Rebecca Roush, along with graphic designers Tom Suarez and Elizabeth Trunkey, crossed the street to Joe's Tavern on Fifth Avenue where, amid the smell of scrambled eggs, cigarettes, and stale beer, they followed the news on live television.

Martin Young had just been promoted to Sounder operations manager. That day his first-ever meeting as manager was convening a command post and security walk-through for protocols in a terrorist attack. "Nothing like baptism by fire," he would later say.[6]

Around the Puget Sound region visitors were barred from the Space Needle and federal buildings as police moved floor to floor checking for suspicious packages. Fearing car bombs, the state ferries accepted only walk-on passengers. Police scrutinized overpasses and tunnels looking for anything suspicious. On a day when the World Trade Center's twin towers in New York came down, everybody looked suspicious and anything seemed possible.

Sea-Tac Airport was shut down but Sound Transit and Metro buses were allowed in and out to rescue stranded passengers. Throughout the remainder of the day transit buses and Sounder trains continued their job of carrying stunned passengers home. There was a feeling on those trains and buses that the world's tectonic plates had shifted and now it was a matter of waiting to see what would happen next.

• • •

In the uncertainty following the attacks, someone decided it was a good idea for Sound Transit's two top security officials, who were not police officers, to wear side arms to work. So the two men, more comfortable behind desks writing memos and reading budgets, dug around at home, dusted off their pistols, and brought them in to Union Station. The weird display of firearms lasted less than two weeks. Sound Transit was only running buses and a few Sounder commuter trains a day between Tacoma and Seattle in 2001, hardly a prime target for terrorists.

The 9-11 attacks had an immediate impact on airline security, but it would take a while for that urgency to translate to transit. It wasn't until the deadly coordinated terrorist attacks on the Madrid commuter rail service in 2004, and then the London Tube and bus attacks in 2005, that attention focused on all mass transit, not just airlines. Big transit systems carrying millions of people provide the potential for large-scale disruption. Because of the volume of riders and number of access points transit systems are difficult to secure. And unlike airlines, there are no inspections before boarding or requirement for identification.

In the aftermath of 9-11, passengers on Sound Transit commuter trains and buses were asked to become the eyes and ears for security, to be aware of people behaving oddly at stations or leaving behind bags and packages. "See Something: Say Something" posters showing shadowy people and packages appeared in train stations. Sounder riders began hearing taped messages on their trains reminding them to report anything suspicious to the conductor or police.

Like transit systems across the nation Sound Transit searched for the right mix between friendly and cautious, a delicate balance that would continue for years.

18

Wait Until Next Year

It's our job to make this happen.
—Greg Nickels

Life moved on in 2001, albeit with the shadow of 9-11 not far from everyone's thoughts.

Around that time construction began on Tacoma Link. Sound Transit called the 1.6-mile project the first light rail line in the state, but more accurately it was a streetcar. No one at Sound Transit was arguing semantics. It was laying tracks for trains and it was the only construction underway in the Link department. The inimitable Henry Cody was put in charge.

"Tacoma actually wanted a project whereas in Seattle we had all this fighting," Cody recalled. "But Tacoma saw this as a great little project of street improvements and a people mover. It was something real and we did it."

Tacoma, forever little brother to the big city 33 miles north, had bragging rights in 2003 when Tacoma Link trains began running long before anything in Seattle. The line quickly became a popular addition to downtown and eventually plans were made to expand into the city's medical district and Hilltop neighborhood. "It kind of showed up Seattle," Cody said. The trains would soon carry nearly a million passengers a year.

Meanwhile, plans for the light rail line in Seattle were also percolating along. In November of 2001, the board officially adopted the route going south from downtown Seattle to Tukwila and eventually Sea-Tac Airport. Two months earlier, before the board's adoption of that route, Earl said she would stake her job and reputation on the accuracy of the plan's budget.[1]

The light rail project received even better news that November when Sound Transit Board member Greg Nickels was elected mayor of Seattle following a campaign where he found himself having to defend the unpopular agency at every turn. His run against Seattle City Attorney Mark Sidran was the closest race for Seattle mayor in nearly a century. Of the nearly 160,000 votes cast, Nickels won by 3,078 votes.

An internal Cocker Fennessy memo celebrated the Nickels victory:

> The election of Sound Transit Board Member Greg Nickels to be mayor places the light rail program on a solid footing to begin construction in 2002. Roadblocks that could have been put up by a reluctant mayor are no longer a concern. The mayor's clout with civic organizations, such as the Seattle Chamber and the Downtown Seattle Association, may also help rally support for the light rail program.[2]

One of Mayor Nickels first meetings was with all city employees working on permits to run light rail through Seattle. Nickels told those staffers they were part of a new era of partnership with Sound Transit. There would be no more waffling or mixed signals coming from city hall, as was occasionally the case under previous Mayor Paul Schell. "From this day forward, understand that it's our job to make this happen," Nickels told them.

The Sound Transit Board also got a makeover. Dave Earling completed his two-year term as chair and gave way to King County Executive Ron Sims. In one of his first acts as new chair, Sims tossed light rail critic Rob McKenna off the board. McKenna's four-year term was up and Sims grabbed the opportunity to replace him with a light rail advocate.

"This is about politics," McKenna told the *Seattle Times*. "Ron [Sims] doesn't want critics or skeptics. He wants board members who will go along with the program."

Sims responded: "I just think we needed to have other voices heard. I don't want to reduce this to the Rob McKenna show."[3]

McKenna said being off the board would actually free him up to be more vocal about light rail. Because, as he said: "I've been fairly restrained, believe it or not."[4]

• • •

While it appeared that Sound Transit had survived 2001 and was chugging into 2002 with a little momentum, the Mariners magical season abruptly fizzled. The team tied the major league record for wins during the regular season, an astounding 116 games, but then the playoffs began. In the American League championship series, down two games to none and heading to New York against the dreaded Yankees, Mariners skipper Lou Piniella guaranteed the Mariners would win at least two of the next three, forcing the series to return to Seattle. It was an audacious boast, particularly coming from the polite Pacific Northwest. But even with Piniella pulling the strings and the play of Ichiro, who was later named the most valuable player in the league, the M's were unable to overcome the Yankees.

Some diehard fans, sifting through the ashes following their loss to the Yankees, believed the 9-11 attacks and subsequent baseball layoff led to the Mariner's demise. While the attacks did seem to break the Mariners season-long momentum, such explanations ignored the obvious roster deficiencies exploited by the talented team from New York.

With the Mariners, as it was with light rail, it would be "wait until next year."

19

Live Another Day

It was like there was a legal minefield.
—Desmond Brown

In a small courtroom tucked inside the old gray King County Courthouse, Joni Earl and Chief Counsel Desmond Brown awaited the fate of their agency. Crisis was common to Sound Transit in 2000 and 2001, but rarely had the future hinged on such a decisive moment. Earl and Brown masked their anxiety with an outward calm.

Throughout Sound Transit's short intense history lawsuits were as regular as train arrivals at King Street Station. Consider that:

There was a lawsuit challenging Sound Transit's authority to collect the sales tax.

There was a lawsuit over construction work in the Rainier Valley.

There was a lawsuit by contractors who wanted more money.

There was a lawsuit to force trains into a tunnel.

There was a lawsuit when Sound Transit refused to run a controversial ad on its trains.

There was a lawsuit claiming a new light rail environmental impact study was needed.

There was a lawsuit to stop trains from running on the I-90 bridge.

There was even a lawsuit from a man who said that work on Sound Transit's light rail line caused a toilet he was inspecting to explode, knocking him to the floor in a flood of filthy raw sewage.

But this one was different. While all those other lawsuits were meant to do damage, Sane Transit versus Sound Transit could, as Brown said, be a "showstopper." Privately, Sound Transit's top management was very worried.

The lawsuit took its name from Sane Transit, the light rail opposition group that had expanded over the years to include influential adversaries such as Emory Bundy and former Sound Transit Board member Rob McKenna, as well as Maggie Fimia, King County Council member, and Nick Licata and Peter Steinbrueck, Seattle City Council members.

The Sane Transit lawsuit, filed in King County Superior Court in Seattle, claimed that Sound Transit exceeded its authority when it changed the 10-year, 21-mile light rail line approved by voters in 1996 to a shorter line that would take at least 13 years to build.

Defending Sound Transit kept Desmond Brown up late at night in his office at Union Station. There, amid his law books, whiteboard covered with notes, and piles of paper, he crafted a defense he hoped would win the legal argument and keep the agency open. He knew he had to be at the top of his game because, as he remembered, the opposing lawyer was very good and was making tough legal arguments. This would be no pushover. The case, he said, "turned on some very arcane points about the wording of the ballot measure and the wording of the plan documents and some…law that was almost 100 years old."

Brown hoped the court would see that by November 2002 Sound Transit had shown itself to be competent, capable, moving on from its early struggles. "We were clearly on the right track and moving ahead and looked like we were a credible solid agency," he said. But would that mean anything to the Superior Court judge hearing the case?

Sound Transit told the court it had the authority to change the route because the ballot measure referred to a "Resolution 75" approved by the board before the 1996 election. That resolution outlined the comprehensive details for implementation, construction, and financing for the regional transit plan before voters. In addition, the agency argued, it gave Sound Transit the authority to make changes to the light rail line in the event of a budget shortfall.

The attorney for the opponents argued that because Resolution 75 was not published in the 1996 voter's pamphlet or in an eight-page flier mailed to households before the election, the agency had deprived voters of key information.

It was not being overly dramatic to conclude that losing this case would have been disastrous to the agency. Or, as Brown deadpanned, "it would not have been a good day."

Losing the lawsuit would likely have required a new election to give the agency authority to proceed with the shorter line. That meant all the light rail planning, hiring, engineering, and public outreach would stop while the agency once again prepared for an election and all its surrounding drama. Following two years of negative news and an energized opposition, there was real concern inside the agency that voters would turn against Sound Transit.

They sat nervously in Superior Court that afternoon in November 2002 awaiting Judge John Erlick's decision. Faces betrayed little emotion as the judge entered the courtroom and began reading his decision. It wasn't until later, away from the reporters and cameras, that Brown, Earl, and other top Sound Transit management would relax and celebrate.

Erlick ruled that the agency had not exceeded its authority and that voters in 1996 had granted the Sound Transit Board discretion to make decisions about how to modify the plan to deal with problems and changing conditions. Sound Transit employees emerged from the courtroom with suppressed smiles. Nearby, the attorney representing Sane Transit announced to the reporters huddled around him that they would appeal the decision "very promptly" to the State Supreme Court.[1]

An hour or so after the ruling, relieved Sound Transit leaders met at F. X. McCrory's, a venerable oyster and chop house in Pioneer Square near Union Station. There, amid the clinking glasses and bustling waiters, cigars were lit and drinks poured. Now, away from the newspaper reporters and Sane Transit supporters, they could relax and ponder how close they had come to shutting down.

Sound Transit, they knew, would live another day.

20

Comeback Kids

I went into tough-mom mode.
—Sen. Patty Murray

Now the only thing keeping Sound Transit from breaking ground on light rail was the long-awaited federal grant. Emphasis on long awaited.

The misadventures began in April 2001 when Norm Mineta, the U.S. Transportation Secretary, put all Link federal funds on ice while the Inspector General's auditors ground through a long, thorough investigation. As months turned to years it seemed as if Sound Transit would have to wait forever to break out the balloons, speeches, and gold-painted groundbreaking shovels.

Sen. Patty Murray, always a staunch ally of the agency, was in a position to help. But the senior senator from Washington State, who first came to Washington, D.C., in 1992 as the "Mom In Tennis Shoes," believed in tough love. Over her decade in the senate Murray had grown enormously in stature and now had great influence. But she saw that the fledgling agency headquartered in Seattle needed to improve if it were to survive.

"I knew that Sound Transit was in trouble," Murray recalled. "I was worried that if Sound Transit didn't get its house in order, public support would continue to dwindle and the project would be at risk. So I went into tough-mom mode. I demanded Sound Transit make serious changes. I put them in time out: No funding until they got it together."

Ric Ilgenfritz, who arrived at Sound Transit after working on Capitol Hill, including for Senator Murray, said that over the years Murray had built up a good working relationship with Norm Mineta, so he listened when she asked him to give Sound Transit time to work through its problems. "You can't undervalue the importance of Patty's contribution because she basically created that buffer from the federal politics that allowed us to retool the project," Ilgenfritz said.

Also important, Ilgenfritz added, was that the state's congressional delegation in Washington, D.C., never flinched. "They were always with us, Norm Dicks, Patty Murray, [Congressmen] Rick Larsen and Jim McDermott. I remember I went to see McDermott on a tour of D.C. right after I started just to introduce myself to everybody and I got like two minutes into my spiel and he said: 'That's enough, I'm with you, you don't need to call me again until you have a ribbon to cut.' Sure enough he showed up at the Link groundbreaking a couple years later."

Away from public eyes, as Sound Transit Board member Bob Drewel recalled, there was a point where patience in D.C was wearing thin. "Norm Dicks is kicking us around and all the folks in Patty Murray's office too because they're getting kicked around back there, so it was not a fun time. Behind the scenes they were grilling the shit out of us."

Back in Seattle, it was clear early on that with the mistakes Sound Transit had made, the Federal Transit Administration would require the agency to go above and beyond to prove its readiness for federal funding. Sound Transit would also have to convince the U.S. Inspector General's tough auditors, as well as a skeptical Bush administration, that it had the people and plan to successfully build and operate Puget Sound's light rail system.

Or, as Ilgenfritz said, "they were basically going to take a belts-and-suspenders approach to oversight."

While Sound Transit languished in self-inflicted purgatory, the steps needed to secure the federal grant were clearly spelled out: The agency must make the changes necessary to receive the FTA's "Record of Decision," meaning it approved Sound Transit's environmental studies for Link; Sound Transit also had to receive permission from the now skeptical FTA to advance light rail into final design; and the FTA would then have to officially approve the final design. Meanwhile, before the project could move forward, the federal Inspector General had to issue its audit report saying Link had turned around and was ready for federal funding.

Clearly, the list of requirements was long and reaching each of those milestones took significant effort. But because the steps were laid out in advance and clearly understood by all, Sound Transit could employ a media strategy that celebrated every milestone along the way. In the politically-charged environment that Sound Transit occupied, showing progress was crucial.

"I remember sitting there and we had the media in the board room and it was one of the first times we said Sound Transit has a major announcement—we didn't say what it was, and in those days you could do that and get four cameras and all the papers," Ilgenfritz said. "Ron Sims was board chair and he's late coming from somewhere else and he's not ready and he says 'OK, what are we saying?' And Joni is telling him what the thing is and he said 'no, what's our sound bite?' And I said well, you could steal from [former President Bill] Clinton and call us the Comeback Kids. And he was like 'Comeback Kids, that's it' and he goes in and lays it down and everybody starts writing. And that was the headline."

• • •

In July 2003, more than two years after the federal grant was put on hold, the FTA officially recommended that Sound Transit receive its $500 million grant. But, of course, that wasn't the end of it. Opponents rolled up their sleeves for one last political maneuver to kill the project. And it involved Karl Rove, President Bush's senior advisor and deputy chief of staff, the most feared political operative in D.C.

After the FTA announced its decision to award the grant, an automatic 90-day congressional review kicked in. Normally, when a project passes through such thorough oversight, the congressional review is a formality. But during that three-month window, Congresswoman Jennifer Dunn, who had fought against the light rail plan for years, tried an end run by taking her case directly to Karl Rove. Dunn represented East King County, home of powerful light rail opponents Rob McKenna and Kemper Freeman, and she herself had influence in the Bush administration. It was a risky gambit, Ilgenfritz said, because at that stage in the game Sound Transit's grant had already been blessed by the Inspector General as well as Norm Mineta, the Bush administration's hand-picked transportation secretary.

Joni Earl was at a conference in Canada when she received the phone call that caused her momentary panic. "I was like 'oh my god Karl Rove!'" Earl said. "I remember saying to a lobbyist one time that I'll be fine as long as Karl Rove doesn't get involved and then I get this phone call saying Karl Rove was asking about our full funding grant agreement and I went 'oh, shit.'"

Earl immediately called Tony Williams, a Republican lobbyist working for Sound Transit in Washington, D.C. and he reassured her: "Calm down, calm down, they've already called me and I told them they're barking up the wrong tree."

According to Ilgenfritz, the story went like this: Williams told Ilgenfritz that a meeting on Sound Transit's grant had been set with Rove for the following week. Unbeknownst to opponents, the ace in the hole for Sound Transit was that the Rove staffer who was preparing him for the meeting was a friend of Williams. That staffer asked Williams, and by extension Sound Transit, to draft the memo that would go to Rove. So, the memo that was eventually placed in Karl Rove's briefing packet was essentially ghostwritten by Sound Transit.

"When (Dunn) went in there and asked him to tube the grant agreement Rove said, basically, not only no but hell no, and why would you even ask?" Ilgenfritz said. "Why would you put the president in the position of having to throw his own people under the bus?"

Meeting over. Game over.

On October 24, 2003, the FTA formally approved Sound Transit's federal funding grant and the next day it officially arrived by email to Earl's office in Seattle. With a handful of agency leaders looking on, she eagerly signed the contract.

Cue the victory speeches. Link light rail construction, finally, unbelievably, was about to begin.

21

In Retrospect

I think our obituary was written more than once.
—Ron Lewis

With light rail trains now an established part of the Seattle landscape and more on the way, it seems impossible there was a time of such peril for Sound Transit. So, how close did the agency come to dying during those early years? Those closest to the flames agree the heat was intense, but not all were convinced it would be fatal.

Greg Nickels, former Seattle mayor and Sound Transit Board chair, said this: "At that crisis point, I think, it could have gone either way. After that it was hard, I wasn't sure *I'd* survive, but I felt the project would survive."

Agnes Govern, former director of ST Express: "I never thought we were done for. I never started looking for another job, I never worried about not making it, but that was absolutely in the air."

Ahmad Fazel, former Link light rail director: "If we didn't get that [*Seattle Post-Intelligencer*] story pulled, I don't think Sound Transit would have existed."

Ron Lewis, Link director: "There were times we were teetering on extinction. If you'd been here at that time, and then left and went someplace else, and came back two years later, it was probably a coin toss if you go: 'oh, that agency that was here a couple years ago is gone,' or 'that agency made it back.'"

Tim Healy, marketing director: "I don't know if it really sunk in that the agency could have gone under. Somebody could have said that's enough, but it's one of the resilient things, maybe it's from the example of the '95 election that you could easily have tucked your tail and said well, they don't want it, but the reality is the people who have always been at Sound Transit have always believed. They were not doing it because it's a lucrative place to work, they were doing it because they believed in what it would do to shape the region, they believed that transit was good, that you were doing something good for the region."

Bob Watt, former Seattle Chamber director: "Yes, I was worried sick for a while. It was pretty bad there for a bit. There were days I was worried the whole thing could crater."

Brian McCartan, former Sound Transit Finance Director: "Politically we were very much on the ropes."

• • •

Regardless of how close the agency came to going under, key people and the right decisions at key moments kept it together, albeit with duct tape at times.

The solidarity of the Sound Transit Board, was one example. If, during its most vulnerable days as Bob Drewel said, just one leader of the board had written a newspaper opinion piece doubting the agency's ability to go forward, that alone might have generated the momentum to kill it.

His fellow board member, Dave Earling, remembers the real fear the agency could collapse. "But we had a meeting amongst the board leadership, we made the judgment that we were going to do what it took to make it work. It was pretty exciting because we all said, 'you know folks, this has to work.'"

Peter Peyser, a D.C lobbyist representing Sound Transit, said without Norm Mineta the agency might have folded. Mineta was the Bush Administration's Transportation Secretary who gave Sound Transit the time to make changes to secure its $500 million federal loan. Without that loan, the project would have died. Mineta, a former Democratic congressman and chair of the House Transportation Committee, was a friend of the Washington State delegation in Congress and also knew many of the players in the Puget Sound region. That helped. "I really think it's part of the good fortune that President Bush appointed him," Peyser said. "Almost anybody else he might have appointed probably would have just said it's done, period. He absolutely could have just cancelled it and said 'I've got another place where I can put this money.'"

Other obvious turning points in the agency's early lifetime included the *P-I* front page retraction and later, winning the Sane Transit lawsuit. A loss in court would have forced a re-election when the agency was at its nadir with voters. If Greg Nickels had lost his bid for Seattle mayor in 2001, crucial city government support for permits and access would have disappeared during a most tenuous time.

Besides the board's support, there was essential unwavering solidarity in the Washington congressional district. Mike Vaska, one of Sound Transit's earliest and strongest proponents, recalled that "Patty Murray and Norm Dicks were the rocks on the federal side of this."

Vaska also credits early leaders like Bob White, who had the skill set necessary to make the transition between the failed vote in 1995 and the successful vote a year later. After the 1995 defeat, many leaders in the region thought light rail was a loser and didn't want to test voters again.

"You need leadership, no question, you need to have the right people in the right position," Vaska said. "But I don't really believe in a messiah in a public project like this."

No messiahs, perhaps, but the closest thing to it in those rocky years was CEO Joni Earl, who gathered together the right team with the right energy to put the agency back on track.

22
Remarkable Ability

She did something that was kind of magical.
—David Beal

Resting on the mantle in Joni Earl's Tacoma living room is a blonde Barbie doll, out of place it would seem, even frivolous for a life of such serious achievement. That is until you learn what it represents.

During the early days it was a custom at Sound Transit to mark special events with employee skits at the regular Wednesday morning all-staff meetings. The skits allowed staff to share a light moment away from the constant negative barrage. So it was over the years that the big Sound Transit board room played host to garish wigs, colorful costumes, a Star Wars sketch, dancers, game shows, bad poetry, and at least one fake TV newscast. What started out as a dry report on a tunnel shaft construction project suddenly turned into a parody of the 1971 movie *Shaft*. Once, when chief counsel Desmond Brown entered the room, over 100 staffers covered their faces with life-size cutouts of his face. Another skit introduced the blonde Barbie doll dubbed the Joni Earl Action Figure. It grew into a tradition among staff to pack that Barbie doll along on vacation. Photos of the doll in exotic places were proof to colleagues back home that the hard-working, sleep-deprived Earl was, at least in spirit, along for the ride.

That was how the Joni Earl Action Figure came to be photographed, in various costumes and poses, in Latvia, a beach in the Philippines, Venice, Croatia, Mexico, in front of the Eiffel Tower, in evening dress before the Bellagio Hotel in Las Vegas, overlooking the Grand Canyon in Arizona, and with a policeman on horseback in Washington, D.C. Eventually, after its worldwide tour, the doll found its way onto Earl's mantle where it sits today, retired.

Rebecca Roush, the relentless organizer of Sound Transit events and spirit behind the travelling Barbie, said it was an acknowledgment of Earl's contributions and a symbol of staff's affection during a very stressful time. It also showed that Earl was not above poking fun at the seriousness around her.

So, what made Earl a leader who was in turn respected by opponents, trusted by community leaders, and revered by Sound Transit employees to the point they would pack, haul, dress, and snap pictures of a Barbie doll on their personal vacations?

Greg Nickels, former Seattle Mayor, said she had a way of earning respect. "She could make tough decisions and people would accept them from her in a way that they might not from other people just because she was so genuine," he said. "Nobody felt there was a hidden agenda. I may not agree with you but I don't think you're lying to me, I don't think you're trying to mislead me, you're genuinely telling what you believe and have the information to back it up. She has a really remarkable ability, I think, that way."

Bob Drewel, former board chair and longtime colleague, believes the way Joni Earl accepted difficult challenges and reacted under pressure is a measure of who she is. Example: In 2007, Sound Transit teamed up with highway advocates to ask voters for $47 billion to improve roads and extend light rail 50 miles. It was a patched together, last-minute plan that was doomed to failure from the start. Six weeks before the election, Ron Sims, the powerful King County executive and former Sound Transit board chair, unexpectedly announced in a *Seattle Times* editorial that he was voting against the measure, creating a fissure in the fragile support for the plan. Transit advocates felt betrayed, including many in the upper reaches of Sound Transit. As Drewel recalled:

> When Ron Sims went south, Joni could have done some really foolish things but what does she do? She picks up the phone and calls him and says 'you and I have got to talk' and by Ron's description read him the riot act. She said 'we're going to have to go forward from this point, I want you to know,' et cetera et cetera, and they got on with it. Most leaders would have called up the balance of the board and said 'I need you to go do this to him.' That's just an extension of how solid she is.

Thomas Shapley, a member of the *Seattle P-I* editorial board that scrutinized Sound Transit over the years, said Earl fit in comfortably with the best state and regional leaders:

There was a level of professionalism and drive and enthusiasm and credibility that was refreshing. She held her own with the board with all those electeds and all their axes to grind and all their allegiances to where they came from. Here she is dealing very well with all these strong personalities, many of them male, all of them with their own political needs and half of them looking for higher office, so it was a tough, tough job but I recall her handling it very well. I don't recall anybody wanting to mess with her too much.

John Niles, a transportation researcher, consultant, and longtime Sound Transit critic, said "I continue to regard Sound Transit's rail programs as a very large public policy mistake, an enormous misallocation of resources with huge opportunity costs." And yet Niles acknowledges Earl's value:

She gets full credit for what ST accomplished on her watch. She was an effective spokesperson for the agency. She managed the scope reduction from the Sound Move promise to the Initial Segment and achieved the first FFGA in the fall of 2003 through some difficult twists and turns. She managed the pivot from tax election defeat in 2007 to a doubling of ST tax streams in 2008. She very effectively kept a lid on the impact of the Great Recession on Sound Transit's prospects for 2009 revenues during the ST2 election campaign of 2008. She hired, managed and retained strong staff people and managed around others that were weaker. Her legacy will be the Central Link train from Northgate to Angle Lake and East Link as well.

Daphne Cross, Earl's friend and longtime senior executive assistant, said simply: "She commands respect when she enters the room."

But added up and put together it was more than all that. There was also the human touch. When you talk with Sound Transit staff they inevitably tick off which of Earl's traits they hold most dear: She listened, she knew everyone's names and backgrounds, she cared, she was smart, pragmatic, had a nose for detail, believed in community service and, unreservedly and unabashedly, loved Sound Transit.

When she was a girl of six or seven Earl would tag along when her father volunteered at Special Olympics track meets. That, and the fact that her elementary school had a wing of special needs kids, made her comfortable and understanding around children with disabilities. Besides the blue collar work ethic, she developed an empathy that would show up later at Sound Transit when she'd personally call or send notes to employees who suffered a loss.

Until she retired from Sound Transit, longtime employee Teri Bubnick kept a handwritten note on her desk. Wherever she moved through the agency it stayed with her as a constant reminder. The note was from Joni Earl and it said, simply, "I appreciate your work and I appreciate you."

"She had a way of making people want to work for her," Bubnick said.

23

Under Her Watch

We're leaving something for our kids, something we can be proud of.
—Ron Endlich

So, how do you measure legacy? At a transit agency, the first measure is performance.

In the year 2000, Sound Transit's trains and buses carried about four million passengers. Today, with Link light rail fully running between the University of Washington to just past the airport, total ridership is approaching 50 million a year.

More than 76,000 passengers ride Link trains every weekday, and they are packed with rush hour commuters and people heading to popular destinations around the city including downtown, the sports stadiums, the University of Washington, and the airport.

But the job is far from finished. Besides operating trains and buses every day, Sound Transit launched a major light rail expansion project in 2016 after Puget Sound voters agreed to tax themselves for an additional 25 years and $54 billion to extend Link to Everett, Tacoma, Ballard, and West Seattle, to downtown Redmond, and between Issaquah and south Bellevue. The 62-mile expansion, added onto the original line and a 30-mile extension approved by voters in 2008, means that when completed, the total 116-mile-long light rail system will rival the best and biggest in the nation.

Fifty-four billion dollars and 62 more miles of light rail. Such a breathtaking expansion was unimaginable in the early days when voters fretted over sinking $3.9 billion into a tiny light rail starter line.

When Joni Earl retired in 2015, the Sound Transit Board brought in Peter Rogoff to lead the agency. Rogoff was former head of the Federal Transit Administration and at one point the third highest ranking official in the U.S. Department of Transportation. He brought his considerable skills and East Coast attitude to Seattle where he would command a massive new workforce of engineers, planners, computer technicians, and support staff needed to map out the 62-mile light rail extension.

The volume and intensity of work was daunting. But even in the new era of light rail, old battles and uncertainties remained. Those with honest disagreements still bristled at how their tax dollars were being spent and weren't about to succumb to light rail's charms. Sound Transit was once again hot enough to rile listeners of conservative talk radio.

The skirmishes were reminiscent of the years 2000 and 2001 or even 1968 and 1970, for those willing to study the past as a roadmap to the future.

Still, unlike the year 2001, now there were 22 miles of light rail up and running and the system had proven itself as a reliable transportation option in crowded Central Puget Sound. A generation of Puget Sounders was growing up riding light rail to classes, the Boys and Girls Club, Mariners games, and the downtown library. There was no talk now about the death of the agency.

• • •

Legacy is also measured in people.

At Joni Earl's retirement party in spring 2016 Sound Transit staffers, some former, some current, some with experience lined on their faces, gathered by the hundreds in Union Station's Great Hall. During the reception a line stretched out before her like subjects before royalty waiting to offer a quiet hello or share a funny or poignant memory.

It was the same Great Hall that 15 years earlier rattled, shook, and was shut down for emergency repairs following the destructive Nisqually earthquake. While restoration experts combed over the Great Hall in 2001, Earl was in her upstairs office working day and night to repair the frayed foundations of the agency itself. Both survived that year, although now at her retirement party it seemed a lifetime ago.

As the program began the Sound Transit executive leadership team, one after another, made their way up a portable stage, took the microphone and reminisced about their former boss. They described her influence, her direction, her integrity, and the way she shaped Sound Transit's image.

Desmond Brown, Sound Transit's head legal counsel, noted how once people sensed that Earl was fundamentally decent, they felt compelled to give her a fair shake, and because of that Sound Transit got a fair shake. "I've heard comments like 'I don't like Sound Transit, but I really, really respect Joni Earl so I have to act decently toward Sound Transit,'" Brown said. "I heard a board member say 'I don't necessarily like where we're going with this, but I'm not going to do anything that Joni wouldn't want us to do.'"

Longtime Sound Transit employees, each in their own way, remembered the arc of her achievements from the shaky beginning where it was mostly dreams on paper to a disciplined organization that opened light rail from downtown to the airport, built an underground extension to the University of Washington, and shepherded through a voter-approved measure to extend light rail another 30 miles.

Clearly the table for future expansion was set under the leadership of Joni Earl. With her in charge, Sound Transit had invested some $8 billion in taxpayer dollars into mass transit improvements across the Puget Sound region including Link light rail and stations, Sounder and stations, ST Express buses, HOV access ramps, and other transit improvements.

Under her watch the agency grew from 261 employees to more than 700. Ridership exploded from one million to nearly 43 million on trains and buses that traveled more than 73,000 miles every day. Her agency commissioned and completed about 100 public art pieces along with 1,500 bike spaces and 14,100 parking spots in stations throughout the Sound Transit district.

By almost any measure, Earl's leadership was an unqualified success.

And yet at her going away party, Ric Ilgenfritz paused in the celebration to address what he called the "elephant in the room."

What was obvious and yet no one wanted to acknowledge, was that the always energetic Joni Earl was now sitting in a wheelchair. It's not fair, Ilgenfritz said, for someone who had done so much to improve the mobility of millions across the Puget Sound region to have her own mobility, her own life changed so dramatically. After all, who at Sound Transit could forget the powerful clack, clack of Joni Earl's high heels on the way into her corner office.

And yet the skills she brought to Sound Transit—singleness of purpose and tenacity beyond all odds—she now brought to her new challenge, which was the daily struggle just to walk.

• • •

When Daphne Cross began working with Earl in 2003 the CEO had an annual appointment with a heart doctor. She told Cross that within the next decade she would need a heart valve replacement. Eight years later it became obvious to Cross that Earl was experiencing stamina problems, but she didn't let many know out of reluctance to be treated gingerly. The indomitable Joni Earl was having trouble walking up stairs without being winded. "But she just plowed on until she couldn't," Cross said.

Unable to delay any longer, Earl left Sound Transit in the winter of 2011 for surgery to replace a defective heart valve. The surgery, although straightforward enough, was not entirely successful. A second surgery was required three years later in January 2014. The email announcement sent to all staff announcing her medical leave in 2014 was brimming with optimism that the CEO would be back soon, rested, fit and ready to go. Essentially, she never returned.

Deputy CEO Mike Harbour took over and he, like everyone else, expected her return shortly. This time the surgery seemed to be working and her recovery progressed. As she built back her strength, Earl's exercise routine included daily walks in her Tacoma neighborhood overlooking Puget Sound. It was there near her home one day that she fell on a sidewalk, striking her head. In that instant her life changed. Ambulance. Emergency surgery. Blood vessel leakage on the brain. The result essentially mirrored the symptoms from a major stroke.

What followed was a long stint in the hospital and then intense rehab that progressed from hospital bed to wheelchair to walker. It was months before she could speak. Cross was the first outside the family to visit Earl in the hospital.

When she began visiting at the Tacoma hospital the nurses asked Cross how she knew the family and how she became a part of Joni Earl's life. She replied that she was Earl's senior executive assistant. "What does she do?" they wondered.

"You don't know what Joni does?" Cross asked, surprised. "They had this dynamic woman there and they never even knew."

• • •

After the hospital Earl worked constantly on her motor skills, slowly learning to speak and then move. As Ilgenfritz once said, you underestimated Joni Earl at your own peril. Her jaw-clenched determination eventually took her from wheelchair to walker to cane where she continued progressing step-by-step. Her voice regained its timbre and expressiveness. She never lost her sense of humor or the nimbleness of mind that allowed her to recall obscure details from decades earlier. By 2019 she was still in physical therapy and determined to reclaim every ounce of strength stolen from her. Success means walking a few halting steps unattended, going to lunch with friends, and enjoying the sunshine of Seattle Mariners spring training in Arizona.

Every so often her husband, Charlie, drives her from their home in Tacoma to Sound Transit where she meets with old friends. As the years passed, Sound Transit was filled with new employees, professional men and women who only knew Joni Earl by name or, perhaps, legend. She was part of the old Sound Transit, the days and experiences that the ancient warriors would recite like stories around a campfire.

Eventually the Great Hall at her beloved Union Station was officially named the Joni Earl Great Hall and a plaque with a few sentences about her was placed on a wall. Although many only know her as that name on a plaque, Ron Lewis said Earl should still inspire today's Sound Transit employees. Her vision and tenacity set the course for a mass transit system that benefits the Puget Sound region every day.

"Others can't be Joni but others can emulate those values and practices she had that made her so effective and that's a huge legacy," Lewis said.

• • •

Legacy also looks to the future.

From the ashes of unsuccessful ballot measures in 1968, 1970, and 1995 to the early struggles of Sound Transit comes a transit system that is poised to carry generations of Puget Sound riders. The light rail line is already woven into the fabric of a region that several times nearly killed it in the cradle.

Those who lived through the beginning refer to the troubles in 2000 and 2001 as the "dark days" of Sound Transit and they sometimes pause to appreciate the struggle because out of it came a stronger foundation for the future.

As Geoff Stuckart, the former Sound Transit employee who was there during the darkest days would remind anyone who would listen: "This is lasting, this is concrete, this will be here for a long, long time. After my kids are gone from this earth it will still be here."

The map showing the full buildout of the Sound Transit system that was approved by voters in 2016. *Courtesy of Sound Transit.*

Acknowledgments

Many people graciously gave their time and memories to make this book possible.

Sound Transit employees and board members, both past and current, patiently answered my questions and reminded me what the Puget Sound transportation landscape was like in the 1980s and 1990s. They include Bob White, Paul Matsuoka, Sheila Dezarn, Dave Earling, Bob Drewel, and Greg Nickels. They are the light rail pioneers for Central Puget Sound.

The leaders who were instrumental in the turnaround at Sound Transit included Ahmad Fazel, Ron Lewis, Agnes Govern, and Desmond Brown.

Rob McKenna and John Niles gave valuable insight from the opposition and Thomas Shapley from an old newspaperman's perspective.

Tom Suarez patiently filled my endless requests for pictures and maps.

Anne Fennessy provided hundreds of documents and records from her years working for Sound Transit. Those documents helped stitch together the region's conversations and concerns about light rail.

And, of course, Joni Earl graciously gave many hours of insight into her thoughts during those early days.

Not everyone agrees about how mass transit and public dollars should be spent, but everyone interviewed for this book had the best interests of Central Puget Sound at heart.

To all, my sincere thanks.

Notes

INTRODUCTION

1. Greg Nickels interview, November 12, 2015.
2. Mike Vaska interview, December 10, 2015.
3. *Seattle Times*, April 6, 2001.
4. *Everett Herald*, March 19, 2001.

CHAPTER 1: THE HOLY GRAIL OF TRANSIT

1. Walt Crowley, "Seattle Voters Reject Plan to Scrap Municipal Streetcars on March 9, 1937," HistoryLink.org Essay 2694, www.historylink.org/File/2694.
2. *Seattle Times*, February 14, 1968.
3. *Seattle Times*, February 14, 1968.
4. *Seattle Times*, November 3, 1996.
5. *Seattle Times*, May 20, 1970.
6. Rob McKenna interview, March 2, 2016.
7. Bob Drewel interview, November 23, 2015.
8. *Seattle Times*, November 1, 1996.
9. David Beal interview, August 13, 2015.
10. Bob White interview, September 27, 2015.
11. *Seattle Times*, July 16, 2011.
12. The Debate over Seattle's Regional Transit System, Harvard Kennedy School, Case Number 1639.0, 2001.
13. Bob Watt interview, February 1, 2016.
14. *Seattle Times*, November 7, 1996.
15. Kathryn DeMeritt interview, January 26, 2017.
16. *Seattle Times*, March 6, 1995.
17. Tim Healy interview, October 27, 2015.
18. *Seattle Times*, November 6, 1996.
19. *Seattle Times*, November 6, 1996.

CHAPTER 2: DON'T SCREW UP

1. Paul Matsuoka interview, September 3, 2015.
2. Brian McCartan interview August 17, 2015.
3. Henry Cody interview, November 13, 2015.
4. Sound Transit press release, May 5, 1997.
5. Desmond Brown interview, October 26, 2015.
6. Agnes Govern interview, September 22, 2015.
7. Walt Crowley and Heather Macintosh, *The Story of Union Station* (Seattle: History Ink for Sound Transit, 1999).

8. Rick Cocker interview, July 27, 2015.

9. Interview notes provided by Cocker Fennessy.

10. Sheila Dezarn interview, October 14, 2015.

CHAPTER 3: TIME TO CALL JONI

1. Hannelore Sudermann, "What I've Learned Since College: Joni Earl '75—CEO of Sound Transit," *Washington State Magazine*, Spring 2010.

2. Anne Fennessy interview, July 27, 2015.

3. Interview notes provided by Cocker Fennessy.

CHAPTER 4: TRAIN TO NOWHERE

1. Thomas Shapley interview, March 2, 2017.

2. Project Review Committee final report, September 27, 2001.

3. Ron Lewis interview, November 5, 2015.

4. Ann McNeil interview, July 29, 2015.

5. Bob White memo to Sound Transit Board, December 14, 2000.

6. Dave Earling interview, August 24, 2015.

7. *Tacoma News Tribune*, November 19, 2000.

8. *Seattle Post-Intelligencer*, December 18, 2000.

9. *The Stranger*, July 12, 2001.

10. *Daily Journal of Commerce*, December 14, 2000.

11. *University Herald*, December 20, 2000.

CHAPTER 5: HOPE WAS NOT OUR FRIEND

1. Deloitte & Touche LLP Performance Audit, September 27, 2001.

2. Rob McKenna, Sound Transit Finance Committee meeting, April 5, 2001.

CHAPTER 6: DARK WINTER MALAISE

1. *Seattle Times*, January 12, 2001.

2. Peter Peyser interview, September 18, 2015.

3. *Daily Journal of Commerce*, January 4, 2001.

4. *Tacoma News Tribune*, January 12, 2001.

5. Dick Falkenbury, *Rise Above it All* (Create Space, 2013), 5.

6. Video recording, Sound Transit Board meeting, January 11, 2001.

CHAPTER 7: SO CLOSE TO DYING

1. Sen. Patty Murray email interview, July 27, 2016.

2. *Seattle Post-Intelligencer*, January 27, 2001.

CHAPTER 8: CHANGE AT THE TOP

1. Marcia Walker interview, September 2, 2015.

2. Bob White resignation letter, January 23, 2001.

3. *Tacoma News Tribune*, January 24, 2001.

4. *Seattle Times*, January 20, 2001.

CHAPTER 9: ARE YOU IN, OR OUT?

1. Memorandum from Anne Fennessy to Joni Earl, March 9, 2001.

2. Geoff Stuckart interview, October 16, 2015.

CHAPTER 10: SHARKS CIRCLING

1. Transportation Legal Defense Fund flyer, 2001.

2. Global Telematics, www.globaltelematics.com.

3. John Niles email interview, April 10, 2017.

4. *Seattle Times*, October 8, 2000.

5. Rebecca Roush interview, February 18, 2016.

6. *Seattle Times*, January 28, 2001.

7. Emory Bundy email to Joni Earl, March 24, 2001.

8. *The Stranger*, October 26, 2011.

9. American Dream Coalition, americandreamcoalition.org.

10. Ric Ilgenfritz interview, October 2, 2015.

CHAPTER 11: PERSONA NON GRATA

1. *Seattle Times*, April 11, 2001.

2. *Everett Herald*, April 15, 2001.

3. *Seattle Post-Intelligencer*, June 23, 2001.

4. *Seattle Times*, February 20, 2001.

CHAPTER 12: TIME TO PULL THE PLUG

1. *New York Times*, March 29, 2001.

2. Inspector General Interim Report, April 4, 2001.

3. U.S. Department of Transportation press release, April 5, 2001.

4. *Seattle Post-Intelligencer*, April 5, 2001.

5. U.S. Representative Hal Rogers press release, April 4, 2001.

6. *Seattle Post-Intelligencer*, March 22, 2001.

7. Joni Earl memo to staff, April 4, 2001.

8. *Seattle Times*, April 6, 2001.

CHAPTER 13: ON THE FIRING LINE

1. *Seattle Times*, March 25, 2001.

2. House Transportation Subcommittee hearing transcript, April 29, 2001.

3. House Transportation Subcommittee hearing transcript, April 29, 2001.

Chapter 14: A Strong Counterpunch

1. *Seattle Post-Intelligencer*, May 4, 2001.

2. *Tacoma News Tribune*, May 5, 2001.

3. Ahmad Fazel interview, September 18, 2015.

4. *Seattle Post-Intelligencer*, May 10, 2001.

Chapter 15: A Near Miss

1. *Tacoma News Tribune*, June 14, 2001.

2. *Tacoma News Tribune*, June 14, 2001.

3. *Tacoma News Tribune*, June 14, 2001.

4. *Seattle Times*, June 19, 2001.

Chapter 16: Hard Pivot South

1. Daphne Cross interview, July 20, 2016.

2. *Seattle Times*, April 13, 2001.

3. *Seattle Times*, September 29, 2001.

4. *Seattle Post-Intelligencer,* December 23, 2001.

5. *Seattle Post-Intelligencer*, October 3, 2001.

Chapter 17: The Daily Slog

1. *Seattle Times*, August 17, 2001.

2. *Seattle Times*, October 28, 2001.

3. Cocker Fennessy memorandum re: Mark Sidran Transportation Action Plan, November 26, 2001.

4. Bruce Ramsey, *Seattle Times,* October 24, 2001.

5. Teri Bubnick interview, April 8, 2016.

6. Martin Young interview, May 12, 2016.

Chapter 18: Wait Until Next Year

1. *Tacoma News Tribune*, September 13, 2001.

2. Cocker Fennessy memo, November 26, 2001.

3. *Seattle Times*, December 29, 2001.

4. *Seattle Times*, December 29, 2001.

Chapter 19: Live Another Day

1. *Seattle Times*, November 11, 2002.

Index

American Dream Coalition, 81–82
Amtrak, 26
Associated Press, 113

Bay Area Rapid Transit (BART), 96
Bay, Paul, 27, 30, 43, 45, 69, 124, 133
Beal, David, 12, 17, 95, 151
Block, Nell, 46
BNSF Railway Company, 18, 23, 26
Boston Big Dig, 105, 109
Brown, Desmond, 26–27, 30, 110, 118, 126, 128, 141–43, 151, 157
Bubnick, Teri, 135–36, 154
Bundy, Emory, 19, 41, 69, 79, 80–82, 110, 141, 165
Bush, George W., 55, 62, 64, 99, 145–46, 149

Citizens for Mobility, 77
Clinton, Bill, 21, 55, 56, 62, 64–66, 98, 146
Coalition for Effective Transportation Alternatives (CETA), 77–78
Cocker Fennessy, 30–31, 38–39, 42, 74–75, 139
Cocker, Rick, 30, 38, 72, 86, 112
Cody, Henry, 25, 43, 60, 129, 138
Collins, Chuck, 57, 79
Community Transit, 26, 54
Condit, Phil, 19, 31, 96, 143
Cranney, Jeri, 44
Cross, Daphne, 127, 153, 158–59

Daily Journal of Commerce, 148
Davis, Aubrey, 15
Dawkins, Mary Ellen, 33
Dawkins, Morrie, 33
Deloitte & Touche LLP, 49, 164
DeMeritt, Kathryn, 17, 20, 95
Desimone, Rick, 62
Dezarn, Sheila, 31, 45, 62–67, 104, 107
Dicks, Norm, 62, 66, 74, 100, 104–106, 121, 145, 150

Downey, Mort, 64–65
Downtown Bellevue Association, 19
Drewel, Bob, 33, 66, 85, 111, 119–23, 145, 149;152; RTA board chair, 17; Snohomish County executive, 9–11, 36, 39–40; Sound Transit Board, 60, 63.
Dunn, Jennifer, 56, 146–47

Earl, Charlie, 10, 71, 103, 122, 159
Earl, Joni, 2–3, 10, 32; Ahmad Fazel, 124–126; congressional testimony, 103–108; court victory, 141, 143; early life, 33–36; FTA grant, 99–100; health issues, 158–59; joins Sound Transit, 38–39; leadership 127, 132, 134, 150, 151–57; named CEO, 118–23; opposition, 80; *P–I* story, 110–116; problems at Sound Transit 41, 43–46, 49, 52; secures grant, 146–48; takes over, 68, 70–75
Earling, Dave, background, 9; federal grant, 66; response to complaints, 84–86, Sound Transit Board member and chair, 21, 42, 47, 60, 63; 68–69, 75, 119–23, 139, 149
Ellis, Jim, 6, 7, 15, 17
Endlich, Ron, 11, 155
Erlick, John, 143
Evans, Dan, 14–15
Everett Herald, 3, 23, 84, 113
Eyman, Tim, 78

Falkenbury, Dick, 58
Fazel, Ahmad, 2, 43, 102, 111–12, 114–16, 124–26, 129–30, 148
Federal Transit Administration (FTA), 56, 63, 97–98, 105, 121, 128, 145–47, 155
Fennessy, Anne, 38, 60, 72–74, 110–13
Fimia, Maggie, 79, 141
Fisher, Ruth, 9, 11, 13, 15

About the Author

Bob Wodnik was Sound Transit's senior communications specialist from 1999 to 2017. Previously a reporter and columnist for the *Everett (WA) Herald*, and a reporter for the *Aberdeen (WA) Daily World*, he was the winner of a *Seattle Times* C. B. Blethen Award for Feature Writing, and a Pacific Northwest Society of Professional Journalists Excellence in Journalism Award.

His book *Captured Honor: POW Survival in the Philippines and Japan*, published by WSU Press in 2003, was selected as a "Best of the Best from the University Presses" by the American Association of School Librarians.

He lives in Everett, Washington.